The Jewish Idea
of Ethics
and Morality

A Covenantal Perspective

Books by Sol Roth

Science and Religion

The Jewish Idea of Community

Halakhah and Politics: The Jewish Idea of a State

The Jewish Idea of Culture

The Jewish Idea
of Ethics
and Morality
A Covenantal Perspective

Sol Roth

THE MICHAEL SCHARF PUBLICATION TRUST
of the YESHIVA UNIVERSITY PRESS
NEW YORK

Library of Congress Cataloging-in-Publication Data

Roth, Sol.
    The Jewish idea of ethics and morality : a covenantal perspective / by
Sol Roth.
        p. cm.
    ISBN 0-88125-951-9
    1. Jewish ethics. 2. Conduct of life. I. Title.
    BJ1285.2.R68 2007
    296.3'6—dc22

                                                    2006101872

                          Distributed by
                   KTAV Publishing House, Inc.
                       930 Newark Avenue
                     Jersey City, NJ 07306
                        www.ktav.com

Table of Contents

Preface

A theory of ethics and morality, if it is a work of logical analysis, must begin with premises that formulate the basic ethical and moral principles that stand at its foundations. Such premises can be drawn from a variety of sources, such as reason, experience, intuition, and society's needs. In the case of Jewish ethics and morality, the premises are to be found in its sacred literature—the Torah, the Talmud, and the Midrash.

By way of methodology, one may adopt what may be called a synthetic approach. This consists of gathering the philosophic positions available on a specific subject, stating one's reasons for accepting some of their elements and rejecting others, locating an unoccupied space in the spectrum of possible theories, and offering what one believes to be a plausible account of one's own views. Alternatively, the methodological option may be that of logical analysis. This consists of choosing premises for the expression of the theory's fundamental concepts, clarifying their meaning by methods of logical analysis and, most important, drawing from them their logical implications. This approach does not require an examination of a range of supporting and opposing theories. It is intended to elicit the meanings contained and often concealed in the premises which are rendered visible by logical analysis. Its purpose is to make clear what one is really saying when one asserts the premises of the theory. This approach can yield new and more profound insights and a fresh and novel understanding of the subject matter.

This dichotomy should not be taken as a claim that philosophers divide into two distinct groups, one of which employs a purely synthetic approach, and the other, one that is entirely analytic. To the contrary, with rare exceptions, both are utilized. I am merely directing attention to a difference in emphasis. Some are preoccupied with comparing and contrasting their views with those of others, and some are primarily concerned with understanding the meaning of their basic concepts and their logical implications.

Accordingly, those who adopt the method of logical analysis generally refrain from elaborate critical analyses of philosophic positions that support or differ from theirs. In addition, their footnotes, except for citing the sources of quotations in the text, are most often utilized to expand on their own thinking rather than focus on the works of others who support or disagree with them.[1] Their paramount concern is the rigor of their logical inferences and the soundness of their conclusions. That is the approach I have adopted in this volume.

I did not wish to be weighed down by the task of explaining and responding to other theories, although in a limited way, I have done that as well in order to highlight elements of the theory I am expounding. My primary goal is to identify what I believe to be fundamental premises of Jewish ethics and morality, and to explicate their meanings by defining them as carefully as possible and drawing their logical consequences. I have always believed, when engaged in my philosophic labors, that this approach is the more rewarding and illuminating option.

My claim to the validity of my conclusions, therefore, is not the preponderance of thinkers who interpret as I do but the compelling force of logic. If others disagree with the premises of my arguments, I have no way of convincing them. For example, if someone believes in the power of human intuition to identify fundamental moral principles, and if that premise leads to conclusions that would not hold in its absence, those who reject the idea of intuitive moral knowledge, as I do, will not be able to accept his conclusions. Or, if someone believes that the covenant, a central concept of Judaism, is to be understood in terms of a contractual relationship with God (bearing in mind that a contract is usually interpreted in terms of obligations mutually and reciprocally assumed) rather than as a one-sided unconditional commitment, a position that I adopt, and if that assumption yields conclusions which would not follow without it, I will not be able to prevail upon him by reasoned argument. A difference of views will generally lead to an agreed-upon conclusion if the disputants begin with identical premises, and perhaps even then not always. In the absence of such mutual understanding, engaging in controversy is usually not philosophically fruitful or personally rewarding. If, however, there are some who accept my fundamental premises and, upon reading this volume, find logical flaws in the analysis or inconsistencies in the arguments, I would welcome their thoughts on the subject.

---

[1] It is worth noting that Albert Einstein introduced only one footnote in his paper on the theory of relativity; Descartes in his Meditations had none; George Berkeley in his Principles of Human Knowledge, five; John Stuart Mill in Utilitarianism, three; and so on. Those who use the method of logical analysis do not require footnotes, though they may introduce some, nor do they depend on documentation.

Introduction

The unique feature of Judaism as a religion is that it is, in all its essential aspects, an expression of the covenant. The covenant is the biblical instrument for the assumption of obligation. It is by means of the covenant that the people of Israel accepted obligations at Sinai. Many were of an explicitly ritual nature, but others were ethical and moral. The moral rules included some that were expressions of the ideals of both justice and mercy. It is important to note, in this connection, that according to midrashic sources, a covenantal agreement was undertaken even before Sinai, while the people of Israel were slaves in Egypt. Its thrust was a commitment on the part of all the enslaved to relate to each other according to the precepts of chesed (mercy).

One of the implications of the covenantal view is the independence of morality from ethics. In the historical development of moral conceptions concerning man's behavior toward man, there have been two major approaches. If we define ethics as did the ancients, Aristotle for example, as the rules of conduct whose observance assures the achievement of happiness, and morality as the set of precepts that guide man's acceptable behavior toward his fellow, we can conclude that there have been two ways of describing the relationship between ethics and morality. One maintains that it is possible to deduce moral principles from the ethical goal. The argument is that if a per-

son conducts himself in accordance with moral precepts, the
achievement of his personal goal, namely, happiness, is rendered more likely. On this view, ethics and morality are interdependent. The other view has it that the principles of morality are entirely independent of ethical considerations. They
ought to be obeyed, not because they are instrumental to
human well-being, but because they are objectively right. This
view, in one of its versions, was expressed by Immanuel Kant,
for example, who was not preoccupied with the ingredients of
happiness but was focused on giving an account of the independent basis of morality. His concern was morality, not happiness. The Jewish view, similar to that of Kant, is that morality is independent of ethics, but for covenantal, not Kantian, reasons. It should be noted, however, that while the two views are
logically independent—that is, moral behavior sanctioned and
motivated by divine prescription is radically different from
conduct justified and prompted by the pursuit of happiness—
there is a relation between them. Responsiveness to divine prescriptions has as a consequence a relationship with the
Supreme Being which translates into joy, a major component of
happiness.

The focus of Chapter 1 is the covenantal agreement undertaken at Sinai and earlier in Egypt and its implications for individual moral behavior and the moral character of the Jewish
community. Chapter 2 examines the additional covenant
entered into by the people of Israel at Mount Gerizim and
Mount Eval following their entry into the land of Israel, in
virtue of which, according to the Midrash, they became guarantors for each other. This undertaking added a crucial dimension to the obligations already accepted at Sinai.

The adoption of the covenantal view required a new
approach to the distinction between justice and mercy. The
usual interpretation is that acts of justice are obligatory and acts
of mercy are voluntary. In view of the fact that the commitment
to perform acts of mercy was undertaken at Sinai, and accord-

ing to the Midrash even before, in virtue of which acts of mercy are equally obligatory, the traditional distinction does not hold. Another characterization of their difference is necessary, namely, acts of justice are responses to individual claims, while acts of mercy, even while obligatory upon the agent, do not imply the existence of claims on the part of individual recipients; the right to such claims belongs to the community. The third chapter is devoted to the elaboration of these concepts.

While precepts of justice and mercy are, by and large, explicit in the Torah, there are many situations that require rules of conduct of a moral sort which are not governed by those that are explicit. For these, another biblical principle, in generic form, is available. "You shall do that which is right and that which is good." But what is the method of deduction applicable to the task of inferring precepts of conduct from this general principle? The fourth chapter explores a utilitarian solution to this problem.

A major objective of this volume is to select a number of fundamental moral and ethical concepts and to exhibit the way they are understood in the perspective of Torah. Some are relevant primarily to ethical concerns, that is, the pursuit of happiness, but can be applied in moral contexts as well. Most, even if they also include an ethical application, are important principally from a moral standpoint, that is, they direct attention to conduct appropriate in interpersonal relations.

Rationality may be viewed as primarily an ethical virtue. It is here defined as the restraint of passion which enables an individual to limit emotional reactions, to conduct his life in conformity with guidelines provided by principle, and consequently to enhance the probability of achieving happiness. Such a disposition is obviously useful in social interactions and also has moral ramifications, but its thrust is essentially ethical. The theme of Chapter 5 is an analysis of rationality in the light of its relevance to meaningful living and human well-being.

The pursuit of excellence, the subject of Chapter 6, on the other hand, is discussed from a moral point of view. It distinguishes excellence from perfection, argues that a vast gulf separates the two, and identifies attitudes, dispositions, and beliefs that are prerequisites to the achievement of excellence in interpersonal conduct and social relations. It is, of course, applicable to ethical objectives as well.

The doctrine that human beings are invested with dignity is central to Jewish thought. It is an expression of the view that human beings possess intrinsic and not merely instrumental value. No other conclusion can flow from the doctrine of man's creation in God's image. Such a belief has implications for man's sense of self-worth, an ethical goal, but even more for his obligation to exhibit respect for others, not so much because of what the other has accomplished but because of what he is. This concept is developed in Chapter 7.

It is my sense that joy is one of the two most important ideas that define the Jewish approach to meaningful living. Two ideas, more than any others, distinguish Judaism from other faiths. One is discussed in the earlier chapters of this volume, namely, the idea of the covenant which establishes that the Jewish community is an obligation-oriented society. The second is joy, to which the eighth chapter is devoted. It is distinguished from pleasure—which itself is not repudiated by Judaism either on religious or moral grounds, if it is sought as an experience consistent with religious guidelines rather than as an end in life—and elaborated in terms of committed relationship with God and man. The pursuit of joy is clearly an ethical enterprise—it is the Jewish version of happiness—but given that it is ultimately dependent on the unselfish quality of relationships, it is, in its human manifestation, a significantly moral concept. The validity of its pursuit distinguishes Judaism from other religions, which teach that a life of intense satisfaction, even in the form of joy, is not the destiny of man in his terrestrial life.

Chapter 9 explores the moral dimension of truth. The question is twofold. First, is there an intrinsic moral obligation to articulate truth in independence of other considerations, such as the consequences of its discovery to mankind? The contemporary debate concerning the public revelation of atomic secrets because of their potential for widespread devastation underscores the significance of this question. Second, is it always morally mandatory to speak the truth? If moral principles were arranged in the form of a pyramid reflecting the relative importance of moral values, would the obligation to speak the truth occupy the position at the pinnacle or one that is subordinate?

The chapter on humility directs attention to the ambiguity of the term in virtue of the fact that it has one meaning when we speak of humility in relation to man and another in relation to God. Humility is not the same as the sense of inferiority. The humble man is one who has outstanding talent, is aware of it, and has accomplished a great deal, the very antithesis of inferiority. In rabbinic literature, humility is regarded as one of the most important virtues, and indeed, a prerequisite to the other virtues.

Reverence appears more appropriate to a religious posture than to one that is moral, and thus one might not normally regard it as a moral virtue. It is nevertheless an essential component of a moral life, because moral principles are, in a religious context, religious. In addition, those who are the object of moral concerns, namely, human beings, possess a religious status, that is, they reflect the divine image, and consequently possess that quality of sanctity which inspires reverence . The religious dimension of moral principles introduces a feeling of reverence that provides the most compelling motivation for moral conduct.

Nevertheless, a question frequently arises concerning the relation of morality and religion. Is moral conduct indeed an inevitable consequence of religious commitment? The question is addressed with regard to religion in general, but there is a uniquely Jewish response. The final chapter attempts to answer this question from the Jewish standpoint.

Chapter 1

The Social Covenant

The people of Israel are *b'nai brit*, children of the covenant. It was by means of a covenant, explicitly described in the Torah, the *brit Sinai*, the Covenant at Sinai, that the people of Israel assumed the obligation to abide by the laws of Moses. According to the *Midrash*, another covenant was undertaken by the Hebrews in Egypt, the *brit mitzraim*, which transformed the descendants of the patriarchs into a people.[1] A second midrash elaborates on the covenant of Egypt

> When the people of Israel was in Egypt, they assembled and lived together in unity, and they arranged a covenant, [assuming the obligations] to perform acts of kindness toward each other, to keep in their hearts the covenant of Abraham, Isaac, and Jacob, to serve their Father in Heaven alone, not to neglect the language of the family of their father Jacob.[2]

---

[1] *Yalkut Shimoni, Deuteronomy* 29:3.
[2] *Tanna D'bai Eliyahu* 23. The fact that they already lived in unity was apparently not quite sufficient for their needs, so they sought a stronger relationship, namely, solidarity, and undertook a covenant to achieve it.

We may identify the *Sinaitic* commitment as the theological covenant, and the one in Egypt as social.[3] It is by means of the latter that they became a people, and by the former a people with a peculiar destiny.

The covenant is an instrument for the assumption of obligations. We need to distinguish between a contractual society and a covenantal society. A contract, in interpersonal relations, is a conditional, mutual, and reciprocal commitment of various persons to each other, an arrangement familiar to all who engage in business affairs. The notion of the contract is also at the basis of the relation of a state to its citizens, at least in a democratic polity. A society based on the social contract, as usually understood in theories of democracy, is one in which citizens are prepared to surrender prerogatives only to receive privileges that are at least commensurate with the prerogatives of which they divest themselves. They are prepared to give only to receive. In such a society, even laws of compassion, when enacted, are based on rights that flow from the social con-

---

Rabbi Joseph B. Soloveitchik directed attention to the distinction between the Sinaitic covenant and the one in Egypt in his essay "*Kol Dodi Dofek*" in *Besod Hayachid Vehayachad* (Jerusalem: Orot, 1976), p. 368. His midrashic source is *Yalkut Shimoni*, and his focus is the difference between the fate and destiny of the Jewish people, whereas the passage here cited is drawn from *Tanna D'bai Eliyahu* and provides the basis for the distinction between the social and theological covenants of Judaism.

[3] Of course, this covenant contained a theological component, but it was essentially social. The undertaking to speak the language of the family of Jacob was clearly intended to adopt a behavioral trait that would preserve the close association of Jacob's descendants. The essential feature of the covenant of Abraham, Isaac, and Jacob was the assurance that the people of Israel would multiply and inherit the holy land, an arrangement whose social consequences are obvious. The sole purely theological element in this covenant was the undertaking to serve God alone, the indispensable underpinning of the totality of Jewish life—social as well as theological.

tract.[4] But Judaism structures the relations of the Jewish people with God and within the Jewish community according to modalities arrived at covenantally rather than contractually. The covenant is an instrument for the unilateral and unconditional assumption of obligations. It differs from a contract, which involves at least two parties and binds each to mutual and reciprocal obligations. A person needs to fulfill his undertakings in a contractual relationship only if the other party fulfills his. A covenant is more in the nature of an oath, which involves an undertaking by only one person or one group; it is one-sided and unconditional.[5] The one-sided, unconditional, and therefore altruistic acceptance of obligation which is of the essence of the covenant clearly applies to all the moral precepts included in the Book of the Covenant, namely, the Torah.

It should be noted that God also undertook covenantal and one-sided obligations to the people of Israel. The best-known example is the *Brit bein Habetarim,* the Covenant-among-the-Parts, through which He assumed the obligation to give to the descendants of the patriarch Abraham the land of Canaan. The covenantal relationship between God and the people of Israel is therefore mutual, in that each has covenantal obligations to the other, but not reciprocal, in that the obligation of each to perform does not depend on the fulfillment of obligations by the other.

Obviously, a covenant, if undertaken by each to all, introduces bonds into their relationship much stronger than those made available by a contract. A contract is sufficient for unity;

---

[4] In the contractual society which is American democracy, social legislation was regarded for a long time as unconstitutional because it was not perceived as necessitated by the social contract. By the end of the nineteenth century and into the twentieth, the concept of the social contract was expanded to include such legislation.

[5] A more complete discussion of the idea of the covenant is available in S. Roth, *The Jewish Idea of Community* (New York: Yeshiva University Press, 1977), chap. 3.

a covenant is indispensable for solidarity.[6] The intent of the covenant in Egypt, drawn by a people already united, according to the midrash cited above, was to ensure solidarity among the people of Israel.

The obligations assumed by the people of Israel in Egypt preceded those undertaken at Sinai, and they consisted, not of *mitzvot*, divine commandments, but of self-initiated undertakings whose implementation would, among other consequences, ensure the preservation and well-being of the people. One of these precepts mandated acts of compassion, kindness, and concern for each other, important commitments intended to ensure the survival of the people in the intolerable conditions of slavery.

The social covenant, like its theological counterpart, is therefore an unconditional commitment on the part of members of the community of Israel to assume one-sided obligations; but unlike the theological covenant, which generated obligations to the Supreme Being, the social covenant was the instrument by which they assumed obligations toward each other.

The Jewish preoccupation with the covenant is an expression of the fact that Judaism is a covenantal rather than a dogmatic religion. A dogmatic religion commands belief; a covenantal religion prescribes action. The people of Israel at Sinai accepted the commandments, which were prescriptions for action, by covenant, and they assumed the obligation to conduct themselves accordingly. Further, the content of a dogmatic theology is intellectual, that is, its adherents are required to contemplate the substance of the proposed beliefs, to understand them to the extent possible, and to affirm their acceptance. A covenantal theology is practical; its theoretical content need not be extensive. The beliefs that are prerequisites to such a theology must be affirmed, but they do not require the depth and detail of comprehension essential to a dogmatic covenant.

---

[6] For an expanded discussion of solidarity, see section II below.

A belief in God, His Torah, and its acceptance by the people of Israel via a covenantal commitment is sufficient, even if the believer does not fully grasp the nature of the Divine Being or even of His covenantal relationship to His people. What is really indispensable in a covenantal theology is an affirmation of acceptance of the obligations to abide by covenantal precepts even if it is accompanied by an unsophisticated belief in God.

Several important consequences that flow from the distinction between a covenantal and a dogmatic religion have ramifications for moral conduct. First, a dogmatic religion gives primacy to principles of faith which it holds to be *true* and therefore mandatory for the belief of all mankind. It thus inevitably becomes missionary in character. An infidel, an atheist, a votary of another faith is denied salvation because he has adopted erroneous beliefs. The dogmatic believer usually maintains that he may coerce another to believe as he does, despite the pain he inflicts upon him, because in so doing he renders his religious adversary an invaluable service. The advocate of a covenantal faith understands that he has the obligation to obey the commandments because he has committed himself to them, but that others who have not made the commitment may refrain from doing so. He sees no profit in engaging in missionary activity and imposing, by threat to life and comfort, a pattern of conduct that a stranger to his community of faith has not voluntarily accepted.

The exponent of a covenantal religion, according to some rabbinic interpretations, need not even require that his religious compatriot entertain true beliefs concerning God. He may regard him as faultlessly religious if, after having affirmed a simple belief in God, he remains obedient to the commandments. This is so even if he adopts religious views that are incompatible with the beliefs of the religion he practices. This point was stressed by Rabbi Abraham Ibn Daud in his critical comment on a judgment of Maimonides, who, in virtue of his rationalistic approach to Judaism, combined elements of dogmatic theology with the covenantal. Maimonides wrote, "Five are in the category of *min* [heretic] . . . [among them] one who says that there exists one God but that He has a form and a shape."[7] Rabbi Abraham Ibn Daud objects:

> Why does he call such a person a *min*? There are some who are greater and better than he who adopted this view because of what they read in the sacred text and even more in the *aggadic* writings which cause false beliefs.

It is important to note in this connection that Rabbi Abraham Ibn Daud was not disputing the substance of the view held by Maimonides, namely, that one who believes that God has a form and shape maintains a view contrary to Jewish fundamental belief, but only his declaration that such a person is a heretic. In a covenantal religion, according to Rabbi Abraham Ibn Daud, it is not mandatory to hold *true* beliefs concerning the *nature* of God; it is necessary to accept and abide by the Torah, the expression of the *will* of God.

There is a contemporaneous debate as to whether Judaism is based on dogma, on a set of beliefs whose acceptance is mandatory for every Jew.[8] Without reviewing the arguments offered in support of the opposing views, it will suffice to say that, at the very least, Judaism requires the adoption of certain beliefs without which, however intellectually attenuated the beliefs may be, covenantal obligations would have no justification, beliefs such as that God exists and that, by means of a covenant,

---

[7] *Mishneh Torah, Hilchot Teshuvah* 3:7.

8 See, for example, David Berger's criticism of Menachem Kellner's *Must a Jew Believe in Anything?* in *Tradition* 33, no. 4.

the people of Israel accepted the obligation to live in accordance with His will as expressed in Torah.[9]

Further, the principles of faith asserted by a dogmatic religion usually relate to the transcendent world. Their focus is the Supreme Being, His attributes, the manner of His revelation, the nature of human salvation, and so on. The mind is, after all, not limited to the world here and now; it has the capacity to wander, and in matters of religion it usually does. A dogmatic religion, because it is essentially intellectual, easily moves beyond the world of space and time in the process of formulating its creed. Judaism did not originally enunciate its principles of faith—its main preoccupation was *mitzvot*, commandments—but when its philosophers and theologians finally did, their formulation of Jewish articles of faith displayed the same transcendental character. The principles of a covenantal religion, on the other hand, are precepts of action— expressed in the six hundred and thirteen commandments that demand performance—and therefore they are readily defined in immanent terms because it is, after all, the physical world that is the realm of human action. This is evident in the case of Judaism, which directs a great deal of attention, in both the Bible and the Talmud, to the elaboration of commandments *bein adam lachavero*, precepts that guide interpersonal relations. And even those commandments identified as *bein adam lamakom*, which mandate conduct in relation to God, for example, observing the

---

[9] It could be argued that Judaism requires of its adherents that they accept beliefs additional to these. A mishnah in *Sanhedrin*, the first of the chapter *Chelek*, enumerates a set of beliefs that need to be adopted by one who seeks a share in the world to come, with the implication that if he fails to do so, he is identified as a heretic. Such beliefs could be regarded as in the category of dogma. An important interpretation of this mishnah is offered by Meiri, who states that all the beliefs it requires are essential to assure that commitment to Torah shall not fade. On this view, all of them are presupposed by the covenant.

Sabbath, fasting on Yom Kippur, have often been interpreted as based on considerations that affect the well-being of the individual and the society to which he belongs. The orientation of Judaism as a covenantal theology is this-worldly.[10]

One consequence of the this-worldly character of the Jewish religion is that a major goal of Jewish life is joy rather than suffering. Other religions may idealize suffering and regard it as possessing intrinsic value. It may be perceived as a purpose of human life in the world here and now, whereas joy and blessedness may be regarded as reserved for the world in the hereafter. Judaism argues otherwise. Suffering in the here and now has value, but only as a means, not as an end.

> And He caused you pain and made you go hungry, and He fed you the manna which you did not know and your parents did not know, to teach you that man does not live by bread alone, but by the words that come from God does man live.[11]

Suffering builds character. It enables a person to contemplate the ultimate purpose of life and to adopt spiritual values as guidelines. The goal of human life, however, is joy. Of course, joy is not to be identified with pleasure; it is not a matter of stimulating the senses or satisfying biological urges. It is rather that sense of well-being and the feeling of elation when one truly finds meaning and significance in human existence. The supreme form of joy is biblically expressed in the phrase "You shall rejoice before the Lord your God."[12]

---

[10] Rabbi Soloveitchik stressed the immanent orientation of Judaism in his *Ish Hahalachah*, in *Besod Hayachid Vehayachad*, pp. 85 ff.

[11] *Numbers 8:3.*

[12] See below, Chapter 10, below for a more elaborate exposition of joy as an ethical ideal.

Nachmanides dramatizes the this-worldly aspect of Jewish life by observing that even on *Rosh Hashanah*, when one would expect the Jew to focus his attention to the fullest on purely spiritual, transcendental concerns, we find him preoccupied with his terrestrial, physical, and economic fate. He writes

> This principle enunciated by the sages that "On *Rosh Hashanah* each man is judged" does not refer to whether he will be deserving of *Gan Eden* and the life of the world to come or of *Gehinom* and spiritual death. For a man is not judged on *Rosh Hashanah* except in connection with this world, whether he deserves life and peace or death and pain. . . . This is the character of Rosh Hashanah. A man's deeds are weighed, and his name is written, and the judgment is sealed reflecting reward or punishment in this world according to what he deserves in proportion to his deeds in this world.[13]

II

Judaism's this-worldly character is also manifested in its preoccupation with social morality. The moral problem is generally formulated in individual, interpersonal terms, that is, What are my duties to other individual human beings? Judaism, however, also directs substantial attention to the social issue of *tikkun haolam*, the improvement of society. The Bible commands the designation of a sovereign, and rabbinic interpreters have noted that his essential mandate and function is social and political.[14] The liturgy of the High Holy Days

---

[13] *Sefer Shaar Hagmul* in *Kitvei Haramban* (Jerusalem: Mossad Harav Kook, 1964), p. 265.

[14] Rabbeinu Nissim b. Reuben Gerondi, *Derashot Haran*, ed. Leon A. Feldman (Jerusalem: Institute Shalem, 1974), pp. 191–92.

includes a passage which speaks of the joy and exultation that will be experienced by the righteous when the kingdom of evil is removed from the earth. The improvement of social conditions for enslaved Jews in Egypt was one of the goals of *brit mitzraim*, the covenant of Egypt. This is also the goal of mankind, in the Jewish perspective, to the achievement of which every member of the Jewish community must exert himself. The socio-moral objective is a central concern of the Jewish covenantal religion.

A social morality is one that is concerned with the definition and implementation of moral norms in a social context. If I return an object belonging to a neighbor, I am practicing individual morality. If I introduce social arrangements, through the creation of institutions, to ensure that the principles of justice will be applied throughout society, I have responded to the imperatives of social morality. The Torah, for example, teaches, "You shall arrange for judges and officers in all your gates," a precept that addresses the moral well-being of the entire community. Dogmatic religion normally focuses its concern on the individual. Even when it encourages the building of schools and hospitals, its primary interest remains the spiritual welfare of the individual and his relation to the transcendent world. Its goal is the salvation of individual man, where salvation is construed in other-worldly terms. Judaism, as a covenantal religion, underscores in addition the importance of building a society whose patterns will embody moral and spiritual values.

Hence, Judaism entertains two conceptions concerning the ultimate destiny of man. One is that of *olam habah*, the world to come. This concept reflects Jewish belief concerning life after death when the righteous find themselves in the presence of the Supreme Being enjoying the state of blessedness as a reward for their personal conduct. The other is *achrit hayamim*, the end of days, a social concept that refers to the time when mankind will live together on earth in justice and peace. The idea of the end of days is as important to Jewish thought as is the world to come.

Crucial moral implications flow from Judaism's social covenant and its emphasis on social morality. The most important is that Judaism is a humane religion which encourages, indeed demands, sensitivity and responsiveness to human beings and the human condition. Other religions also require a display of concern for mankind, but that demand is usually expressed in spiritual, transcendental terms. Judaism directs attention to the painful and often tragic nature of the human existential condition in its terrestrial life. A preoccupation with the transcendental aspects of religion will often prompt theologians to interpret man's good exclusively in terms of salvation in the beyond. The fate of man on earth will not be a central preoccupation. A covenantal religion, which inevitably focuses on social as well as individual morality, will pay greater attention to pain, hatred, and injustice and attempt to create a redeemed society in which all will live in justice and peace. Its goal of redemption will equal in importance that of salvation.

The Jewish sense of social obligation also strengthens the sense of solidarity within the Jewish community. The unity of the Jewish community is not a goal that adequately serves the Jewish social objective. Unity can be achieved by a collection of individuals living and interacting in a contiguous domain when they are driven by a common purpose. The people of Israel suffering a life of slavery in Egypt were united in their struggle to survive the tribulations of their intolerable condition. It was the judgment of the sages that this was not quite sufficient if Jewish continuity was to be ensured. What was needed in addition was the development of a sense of solidarity rooted in the resolve to interact with loving-kindness and, even more, in the capacity to empathize with each other so that the suffering of one becomes the suffering of all. Accordingly, the view that the sole preoccupation of the religious personality is to achieve spiritual involvement with God is sufficient for the development of a sense of unity among those who share the same religious objective, but it fails to achieve the goal of empathy with a specific religious community. If personal salvation in the world beyond is the central, if not the exclusive, religious objective, compassion for the ill and oppressed may well be regarded as a response with theological significance, that is, as a means of serving God and enhancing involvement with Him, but it will not foster communal cohesion and connectedness. It is otherwise with a people which perceives the strengthening of their community and its everlasting perpetuation as itself a covenantally mandated goal of paramount religious significance. The people of Israel were in need of solidarity, and indeed solidarity has been a character of this people across the ages.

The concept of *am yisrael*, the people of Israel, needs to be understood not merely in terms of unity but in terms of the solidarity rendered feasible by the covenant. First, it is important to note the centrality of *am yisrael* in the spectrum of Jewish religious values. The status of the *people* of Israel has not received adequate attention. The importance of Torah, the land of Israel, and for large segments of the Jewish people, the state of Israel, has been recognized, but the concept of the *people* of Israel has suffered unjustifiable neglect. It may be a consequence of the ideological conflicts, divisiveness, and even hostility that have afflicted the community of Israel in recent generations. It needs to be noted, therefore, that the preeminence of the *people* of Israel in the scale of Jewish values is affirmed by the Torah. By way of introducing the Covenant-among-the-Parts, God said to Abraham, "Look to the heavens and count the stars if you can count them; . . . so shall your offspring be." And again later, "I will arrange a covenant between Me and you, and I will make you exceedingly numerous." The clear intent of these divine commitments is that the descendants of Abraham shall constitute a people. If this were not the case, the emphasis on the quantitative dimensions of Abraham's descendants rather than on the spiritual character of each of his descendants, rooted in an Abrahamic relation with God, would be beyond comprehension.

Even the covenantal commitment at Sinai had special implications for marking the descendants of the patriarchs as a people. The Torah is explicit on this score. When, at the end of their forty years of wandering in the desert and prior to their entry into the Holy Land, the people of Israel were once again about to commit themselves by covenant to the Torah, Moses declared, "This day, you have become a people." The declaration does not say that on this day, in virtue of your acceptance of the commandments, you involve yourselves in a special and exalted relationship with God, but that on this day, you become a *people*.[15] Even the Torah, the supreme expression of God's will and the quintessential manifestation of the divine on earth, is herewith characterized in terms of its function in the process and evolution of Israel as a people. The covenant, therefore, was essential to the task of creating and solidifying the people of Israel.

But further, extraordinary importance is assigned to the *people* of Israel through the biblical use of the instrument of the covenant in connection with certain *mitzvot*. The *mitzvah* of circumcision and that of living in and developing the land of Israel are included among the obligations accepted at Sinai, subsequently again in the fields of Moab and at Mount Gerizim and Mount Eval. If nothing more had been done to direct attention to these commandments and to emphasize their impor-

---

[15] *Deuteronomy* 27:9. This declaration was particularly appropriate for the occasion on which it was uttered. The people were about to enter the land of Israel and, immediately before doing so, were required to recommit to Torah. Both the land and the Torah were essential to the goal of establishing the descendants of Abraham as a people.

tance, they would be obligatory in light of the fact that they are included among the six hundred and thirteen commandments. Nevertheless, they are distinguished by the circumstance that a special covenant was drawn for each of them in addition to the generic covenants at Sinai, the fields of Moab, and the two mountains. These additional covenantal commitments introduced greater cohesiveness into relationships within the Jewish community. Further, rabbinic sages declared that covenants not explicitly described in the Torah were also established. One of these was, as already noted, the covenantal commitment adopted by the Hebrews while slaves in Egypt to treat each other with *chesed*, mercy. It is reasonable to conclude that these special covenantal *mitzvot*, biblical and rabbinic, were assigned this extraordinary status because they are indispensable to the goal of establishing the descendents of the patriarchs as a people whose character would be, not merely one of unity but of solidarity. Circumcision gave the people of Israel a special trait by which they could be identified. The possession of a land, the mutual undertaking to exhibit love, concern, and compassion, manifestations of *chesed*, all have as an effect the shaping and strengthening of the bonds among the people of Israel.

III

Another consequence of the concept of the covenant in general and of the social covenant in particular is the Jewish emphasis on the act as an essential factor in the determination of the moral and spiritual quality of an action. In evaluating the moral and religious significance of an act in the Jewish perspective, two elements need to be taken into account—the intention and the action. This is an unusual approach. In ethical theory, the action of the agent, indispensable though it may be to moral behavior, is generally not itself a determinant of moral worth. An act must obviously be performed if the question of its moral quality is to be raised, but the factor which is the determinant of moral value is not the act but the intent that precedes it, or its consequences. The school of ethics which maintains that it is the volitional component that is crucial argues that moral quality depends on motive alone. Its most outstanding exponent is Immanuel Kant, who declared that only an action motivated by a will that obeys exclusively the voice of conscience (the categorical imperative) is to be considered moral. This theory may be contrasted with the utilitarian, which maintains that moral quality is a function solely of the consequences of the act. The argument is that if an act produces a balance of pleasure, that is, more pleasure than pain, it is to be considered moral. In sum, one view claims that it is the intent of the agent that determines moral quality, and the other maintains that it depends on results. Judaism holds that the act itself needs to be taken into account as well, because it, in addition to the intent, contributes to the moral character of an act.

An act that coincides with the form of an action biblically prescribed may have positive moral value even when unaccompanied by a variety of intent that expresses concern for another. The issue of intent arises, in the Talmud, in connection with actions that have a moral as well as a nonmoral, uniquely religious character. On one view in the Talmud, *mitzvot*, that is, biblical commandments of both varieties, the moral and the uniquely religious, do not require *kavanah*, the intent to perform the commandments for the purpose of complying with *mitzvot*. And even Maimonides. who on one interpretation maintains that such intent is an essential prerequisite to the fulfillment of *mitzvot*,[16] grants that there are instances where such intent is inessential.[17] The deed itself, independent of moral purpose, has moral and therefore religious value.

---

[16] *Mishneh Torah, Hilchot Shofar* 2:4. This is the interpretation of the *Maggid Mishneh*. R. Avraham, son of the Rambam, in his Responsa (#9), claimed that in his father's view, intent is inessential to the performance of *mitzvot*.

[17] *Ibid., Hilchot Chametz U'matzah* 6:3.

Judaism, of course, is not altogether indifferent to moral intent. An act accompanied by the appropriate intent has much greater moral significance than one from which intent is absent.[18] Further, there are occasions when, according to some talmudic sages, intent itself carries moral weight even in the absence of an action. The School of Shammai teaches that *makhshavah kemaaseh*, "The intention is like the deed."[19] The intent to steal an object accepted from a neighbor for safekeeping is tantamount to theft. There is even more agreement on the application of this principle, in certain contexts, in relation to the sacred domain. One who, in the process of preparing an animal for sacrifice, specifically the act of slaughtering, contemplates an intent to consume its meat beyond the place or time in which partaking of the sacred food is permissible,

---

[18] Of course, both moral precepts (those that guide interpersonal relations) and those that are uniquely religious (those that involve man's relation to God) are divinely ordained. It might be suggested, however, that while the principle that *mitzvot tzarichot kavanah* (i.e., that the satisfactory fulfillment of precepts requires intent) is applicable to our obligations in relation to God, it is not relevant to moral imperatives. This might be inferred from a passage in the Talmud (*Pesachim* 8a) which declares that if a man were to contribute to *tzedakah* on condition that his son shall live or that he shall enjoy the rewards of the world to come, he is a complete *tzaddik*. In such a case, the intent appears to be faulty and inadequate. Nevertheless, the Tosafists and Meiri explain that he is a *tzaddik* because even if his prayers are not answered, he does not regret his charitable gesture (the Tosafists) and he accepts the decision of the Almighty (Meiri). It is clear that the right motivation enhances the quality of even the moral *mitzvot*

[19] *Kidushin* 42b. *Machshavah* and *kavanah* can both be translated as "intent." but they are of different kinds. *Kavanah* focuses on the *motivation* that prompts the action. It may be a response to the will of God, in which case the agent is credited with the right *kavanah*, or a concern about his own interests, in which case the intent is flawed. *Machshavah*, on the other hand, refers to the *decision* to act or to refrain from acting. A person may decide to act (i.e., he has *machshavah*), but if he does it for personal profit, it lacks *kavanah*.

thereby renders the animal unfit.[20] Rav Assi offered a generalization with regard to positive commandments. He declared, "Even if an individual intended to perform a *mitzvah* and was forcibly prevented from doing so, he nevertheless receives credit as if he had performed it."[21] Notwithstanding, it is a distinctive character of Judaism that it assigns considerable importance to the act in evaluating its moral and spiritual value.

An additional observation with regard to Judaism's emphasis on the performance of the *act* is, however, essential. If an act itself, deprived of the intent to perform it in compliance with biblical and rabbinic prescription, is to be considered moral, it must be accompanied by another kind of intent—not the intent to respond to an obligation, but to perform the *act*. If the intent is lacking entirely in moral purpose, for example, if a generous donor performs his act out of a visceral need to enjoy the appreciation of the community or to derive satisfaction from the knowledge that he is superior to the unfortunate recipient, rather than because of a commitment to the *mitzvah* of *tzedakah*, it is still to be characterized as moral because it had the form of assisting the poor—that is, the individual did give a sum of money to one in need, and the intent to perform the act was present. There is, however, a talmudic category termed *mitasek*, which refers to an act performed unaccompanied by the intent to do so, which is not assigned any moral or religious significance. If a wealthy individual discards coins in the presence of some people suffering from poverty in order to amuse himself, and the coins are collected by an individual whose impoverished condition is thereby eased, however temporarily, the act is not praiseworthy, because it is morally flawed. It lacks both kinds of intent—the intent to perform the act, and the intent to comply with a commandment.

---

[20] *Zevachim* 13a.
[21] Kidushin 40a.

Chapter 2

The Guarantor*

Areivut is a biblical concept that assigns to the Jew the role of a guarantor. *Areivut* is not a *mitzvah*, a commandment; it is rather a state of affairs, deriving from a covenant, in addition to the ones at Sinai and in the fields of Moab, that was established at the mountains of Gerizim and Eval in the land of Israel. The new feature introduced by this covenant is that every Jew is a guarantor for every other Jew. While biblical covenants, including the covenant at the two mountains, refer primarily to a relationship between the Jew and the Divine Being, the focus of the latter covenant is the obligation that a Jew assumes toward individual members of the Jewish community. In this sense, *areivut* is a moral concept because it refers to interpersonal obligations. This covenant therefore, in effect, translates a commitment to the Supreme Being into obligations toward members of the Jewish community.

In our attempt to extract the meaning of *areivut*, no distinction will be made between moral and specifically ritual commandments. The covenantal status of the guarantor requires that he assume responsibilities toward others with respect to their performance of both moral and the ritual obligations, and that this responsibility, since he assumes it toward others, is moral even when he undertakes initiatives to assure that they will fulfill ritual obligations. To assist an individual in the performance of a precept that is obligatory upon him, for example the *etrog* and *lulav* during the festival of Sukkot, is to perform a moral act.

There are varieties of moral imperatives. Many refer to obligations that are ever present and incumbent upon all in relation to every member of the *human community*, for example, not to steal and not to kill. Some arise out of a gesture of commitment in interpersonal relations and are not obligatory upon those who are distant from it. A person can assume moral obligations toward a designated individual, for example, the mutual obligations of a husband and wife or the acceptance by a borrower of the obligation to repay his debt. Similarly, there are special obligations of Jew toward Jew that occur in the context of the *Jewish community*, which are not relevant to those beyond its boundaries, and which are moral in an analogous sense. Among these, are the obligations of the guarantor. What are they?

I

The popular interpretation of the principle of *areivut*, namely, "All Jews are responsible one for another," is substantially, though not entirely, incorrect. To clarify its meaning, we ought to begin with the passage in the Talmud where this principle is explicitly enunciated.

It is written, "and one man shall stumble because of his brother," [this means that] he shall stumble because of the sins of his brother. From this we may infer that all Jews are guarantors (*areivim*) one for the other.[1]

---

* This chapter is an expansion and minor modification of a paper in Hebrew included in a memorial volume in tribute to Rabbi Shlomo Goren on the occasion of his first *yahrzeit*.
[1] Shevuot 39a.

The Talmud explains that this principle is applicable only in instances where it is in one's power to prevent the transgression but fails to do so.

It appears that the focus of the principle of *areivut* is essentially punishment. If an individual refrains from exerting influence upon another to prevent his transgression, then he will suffer the consequences of the other's sin. This interpretation is enforced by another talmudic passage.

> [It is written] "That which is concealed belongs to the Lord our God, and that which is revealed belongs to us and our children (*lanu ulevoneinu*) forever (*ad olam*)." Why are there dots above the words *lanu ulevuneinu* and the *eyin* of *ad*? From this we may infer that they were not punished for that which was concealed until they crossed the Jordan. These are the words of Rabbi Judah. Rabbi Nehemiah challenged: Were they ever punished for those which were hidden? . . . . rather, just as they were never punished for those that were hidden, so were they exempt from those that were revealed until the people of Israel crossed the Jordan.[2]

The phrase "until they crossed the Jordan" is explained by Rashi as follows:

> They heard and accepted the blessings and curses at Mount Gerizim and Mount Eval, and they became guarantors one for the other, as is explained in the tractate Sotah (37b); immediately they were punished, one for the sins of the other.

As has already been noted, the obligations imposed by *areivut* did not take effect until the covenant was once again

---

[2] Sanhedrin 43b.

accepted by the people of Israel, following their entry into the Holy Land, at Mount Gerizim and Mount Eval. This acceptance marked the addition of something novel, a new dimension, if you will, to that which had been undertaken by covenant earlier at Sinai and in the fields of Moab. The novel component was an essential element in the doctrine of *areivut*, namely, that one person can be punished for the sins of another if, when capable of doing so, he fails to prevent them.

The principle of *areivut*, therefore, is clearly one that has to do with punishment; but it is more; it also assigns obligations, and this should not surprise us. The concept of *areivut* in the spiritual realm parallels what obtains in the domain of monetary transactions. An *arev*, a guarantor, is one who assumes an obligation to pay a lender if the borrower defaults. The *arev*, therefore, is one who accepts obligations and is prepared to take the consequences of a friend's failure to discharge his responsibility. The assumption of obligation is also essential to the concept of *areivut* in the realm of spirit. This is confirmed by rabbinic commentary on other passages of the Talmud.

Ahavah the son of Rabbi Zera taught: With regard to all blessings, even if he has fulfilled his obligation [to recite them], he may fulfill the obligations of others [by reciting the blessings for them], with the exception of the blessing over bread and the blessing over wine, in which instance, if he has not yet recited them for himself, he may do so for others, but if he has already fulfilled his obligation, he may not recite them for others.[3]

The rabbis explain that there is a difference between *birchat hamitzvah*, a blessing recited in conjunction with the performance of a *mitzvah*, and *birchat hanehenin*, a blessing that precedes an act of enjoyment, such as the consumption of bread

---

[3] Rosh Hashanah 29a.

and the drinking of wine. In the former case, one may recite a blessing for others even if one has already fulfilled the *mitzvah* for oneself because, as Rashi explains, all Jews are guarantors one for the other. In the latter instance, since the principle of *areivut* is irrelevant, in view of the fact that a *mitzvah* is not being performed, once a Jew has satisfied his obligation to recite a blessing, he may no longer do so for another.

It is clear that in this talmudic distinction, the principle of *areivut* is not used for the purpose of assigning punishment; it is intended to direct attention to obligations. This principle is taken to declare that all Jews have the duty to prevail on others to fulfill the *mitzvot* of Torah; thus they may continue to recite the blessing that introduces a *mitzvah* for another in the event the other has not yet discharged his obligation to do so.

What is the source of the obligation of the guarantor? Two answers are possible: (1) It derives from explicit *mitzvot* of Torah, such as, "Love your friend as yourself" or "Rebuke your friend." If you see another Jew deviating from the path of Torah, your obligation to love and to chastise should prompt you to intervene in order to restore him to the path of righteousness. By doing so, you discharge your duty as a guarantor. (2) The guarantor's obligation is based on the very *mitzvah* he is trying to assist, or to persuade, another to fulfill. For example, when a Jew has performed the *mitzvah* of the *etrog* and *lulav* on Sukkot, or has fulfilled his obligation to give charity, he is not yet relieved of the responsibility that derives from these commandments so long as it is possible for him to influence others to fulfill these *mitzvot*.

While both these interpretations have been articulated by the more recent interpreters of the Talmud, it may be argued that it is the latter interpretation that is the more cogent.[4] In

---

[4] How the rabbis interpret the meaning of *areivut* may also be inferred from the following halachic discussion: If a person is deaf but not dumb (in which case, performing the *mitzvah* of the *shofar* is

truth, if the obligation of the *arev* was assumed by covenant at Mount Gerizim and Mount Eval (as maintained by the passage cited above) long after the people of Israel accepted the Torah

---

beyond his capacity, since the *mitzvah* requires that the sound of the *shofar* shall be heard, and he is incapable of doing so), may he blow the *shofar* for another who is obligated? If the *mitzvah* of *areivut* has its source in the biblical imperative to rebuke a transgressor, then his auditory deficiency should be no obstacle to assisting his neighbor in fulfilling this *mitzvah*. The fact that he cannot hear the sounds of the *shofar* should not be construed as an impediment to helping another satisfy the requirements of this biblical imperative. If, on the other hand, *areivut* means that one continues to be obligated to perform a specific *mitzvah* even after discharging the obligation it imposes, then if, because of incompetence, one is free of the obligation of that *mitzvah*, one cannot fulfill it for another.

On this issue, Rabbi Joseph Karo writes: "A deaf person, even if he speaks but does not hear, cannot satisfy the obligation of others [by blowing the *shofar* for them] because, in view of the fact that he does not hear, he is not a person with an obligation [to hear the *shofar*]. (Orach Chayim 589:2).

In the *Mishnah Berurah* (whose author is Rabbi Yisrael Meir Hakohen), we find the following explanation of this passage: "In the blessing, after all, we recite 'and He commanded us to hear the sound of the *shofar*.'" The implication is that since the one who blows does not have the obligation, because of auditory incapacity, he may not recite the blessing which declares "He commanded us," and consequently cannot function as an *arev* to perform the *mitzvah* for another.

It should be noted that another opinion is offered by Rabbi Yoel Sirkes in his commentary on the *Tur* entitled *Bet Chadash* (*Bach*). He maintains that, in these circumstances, the deaf person may blow the *shofar*. He does not, however, base his argument on the view that the obligation of the *arev* derives from the *mitzvah* of rebuking a neighbor, but rather that the deaf person can satisfy his own obligation by blowing even though he does not hear the sound of the *shofar*, that is, the *mitzvah* of the *shofar* is not limited to hearing its sound and can be performed, though not in an ideal way, by blowing. He is therefore obligated and can function as an *arev*.

and its *mitzvot* at Sinai, among which is included the *mitzvah* of rebuking a neighbor, it would be difficult to accept the view that the principle of *areivut* is based on one of the explicit *mitzvot* of Torah. If it were, why should *areivut*, based on the duty to rebuke, not have taken effect simultaneously with all the other *mitzvot*? Why was the obligation delayed until another covenant was drawn at Gerizim and Eval? It would seem more reasonable to assume that the added feature undertaken after they crossed the Jordan is that every person shall regard every *mitzvah* as imposing an obligation upon him to discharge it not only for himself but for others.

Further, the talmudic passage cited earlier declares that *areivut* is relevant only to blessings connected with *mitzvot*, not to those recited prior to the enjoyment of the things of this world. If, however, *areivut* means that we must assist another in the fulfillment of his obligations, and this requirement derives from the *mitzvah* of rebuke, why should we not be allowed to recite the latter variety of blessings for another? We are, after all, obligated to ensure that another shall recite the appropriate blessing prior to eating, for example. The answer obviously is that while we indeed ought to try to persuade him to say the relevant blessing even if we have to recite it with him, we cannot do it for him. We can serve as a surrogate only in those instances where we continue to have the obligation of the specific *mitzvah*, that is, when we are *areivim*.

We may conclude that the principle of *areivut* is not essentially one which makes all Jews responsible one for another. Such responsibility existed before the introduction into Jewish life of the principle of *areivut*. It was made explicit in the Torah in the *mitzvot* "Love your friend as yourself," "Rebuke your friend," and several others. This obligation dates back to the very gesture of accepting the Covenant at Mount Sinai. The people of Israel were addressed in the singular—"Thou shalt not kill," "Thou shalt not steal," and so on—but when the people responded, it was in the plural—"We shall obey, and we shall listen." In the very act of accepting the Torah, Jews assumed responsibility for each other.

The thrust of the principle of *areivut* is to impose on Jews a subsidiary obligation with respect to *mitzvot*. On one level, every Jew is obligated to perform all of them. On another level, every *mitzvah* imposes on each Jew the obligation to see to it that others in the community also fulfill that *mitzvah*. The result is that every Jew has a dual obligation with respect to every *mitzvah*—one that is personal and self-directed, and another that is communal and other-directed. But in every case, the source of these obligations is the covenantal commitment. The one at Sinai obligated him to perform each and every *mitzvah*; the one at Mount Gerizim and Mount Eval obligated him to prevail on others to perform that *mitzvah* and to be prepared to accept punishment if he failed to intervene when it was possible for him to do so. It follows from this discussion that *areivut* is a principle that assigns to every Jew the status of a surrogate for every other Jew.

II

Ritva (Rabbi Yom Tov Alashbili) concluded that, as a consequence of the principle of *areivut*, the Jewish community should be perceived as one single, unified, integrated entity. He wrote, "All Jews are guarantors one for another; *they are all like one body* [emphasis added] and like a guarantor who pays the debt of a friend."[5]

There are varieties of unity. There is unity of purpose, as exemplified by a nation that consists of different ethnic and religious groups adhering to diverse creeds and distinguishing lifestyles, but are unified based on a common commitment to the political ideals of the nation in which they reside. There is a stronger unity that derives from organization, where the dif-

---

[5] *Chidushei Haritva* on Rosh Hashanah 29a.

ferent segments of a community are assigned different functions and are so coordinated that a designated purpose is rendered easier of realization. Such is the unity of an army, whose
segments receive specific assignments with the aim of achieving a coordinated force, the more readily to accomplish the goal
of military victory. There is also the unity of an organism, characteristic, for example, of a human body. It too has a purpose—
it is a teleological entity; it too is highly organized, but it contains, in addition, the kind of relationship among its components that renders the well-being of each dependent upon the
well-being of the others.

It is this kind of organic unity that Ritva assigns to the
Jewish people. In truth, the *halachah* requires that the people of
Israel shall experience such unity on two levels, that is, it
should be perceived as characteristic of both its physical and its
spiritual existence. With respect to the body, it means that
when one part of the organism is ill, the entire body is affected,
and when one part suffers pain, it is experienced by the entire
organism.

The Talmud puts it this way:

When the community is suffering pain, let not a man say,
"I will go to my home, I will eat and I will drink, and my
soul will live in peace." . . . rather a person shall suffer
with the community, as we find in the case of Moses our
teacher, who shared the pain of the community. As it is
written, "and the hands of Moses were heavy, so he took
a stone and placed it underneath himself, and he sat on
it." Did not Moses have one pillow or one blanket to sit
on? But Moses said, "Because the people of Israel is in
pain, I too will share their pain."[6]

---

[6] Taanit 11a.

It should be noted that the organic unity of the body of the Jewish people, according to this talmudic interpretation, is not a natural state of affairs but results from a halachic imperative. A Jew need not automatically experience pain when his compatriots suffer. It is rather a moral attitude, a posture that Judaism urges upon the members of the Jewish community. It is of course possible, even desirable, that in the process, its members will achieve a condition where the painful response is immediate and habitual, where it is more in the nature of a causal effect than a deliberate response. Indeed it is worth noting that the Jewish people have gone very far in achieving this state of affairs. They have succeeded, in significant measure, in transforming that which according to talmudic principle is essentially a moral obligation into a natural state of affairs. Jews today do not merely perceive an obligation to share the pain of fellow Jews; they do, in fact, experience such pain. Such a relation between Jew and Jew parallels the relation among the several organs of a body. For both, pain in one part is experienced as well by other parts. This is the essence of organic unity in the physical sense.

The halachic situation, however, is different with respect to the spiritual life of the Jewish people. It is also a feature of a human organism that if one of its parts, a hand for example, commits a crime, any other appendage of the same body cannot plead innocence on the grounds that it is the hand that is guilty. This indeed is the essence of the talmudic principle of *areivut*, which expresses the view that the people of Israel is like one body, but in a spiritual sense. A Jew is guilty for the transgressions of others if he could have prevented them but failed to do so. Further, here we are not presented with a prescription to the effect that every Jew ought to regard his soul as organically related to the soul of every other Jew. Rather, it is a halachic declaration, in view of the covenantal obligations undertaken at Mounts Gerizim and Eval, that this intimate, mutually interdependent relationship in fact exists.

The concept of organic unity constitutes a further elaboration of the character of solidarity that is descriptive of the people of Israel. It has been argued in these pages that solidarity is rooted in the circumstance that the people of Israel is a covenantal community. It may now be added that it is the covenant which conferred upon the people the character of an organic entity that transformed the unified people of Israel into a community of solidarity; and that the covenant which more than the others is the source of its solidarity is the covenant at the two mountains.

The rabbis frequently directed attention to the organic unity of the Jewish people in such a way as to make it possible to perceive the people of Israel, in a spiritual sense, as one cohesive entity. In fact, recognizing the physical separation and distinctiveness of each human being, some preferred to interpret this cohesion as existing in the *transcendental* rather than the immanent domain. The Netziv, for example, on the biblical phrase *Yaakov chevel nachlato*,[7] which he interprets as "Jacob is the rope of His inheritance," writes:

> The totality of the people is comparable to a rope which is woven of many strands. . . . Just as a thick rope which has tens of thousands of thin strands is braided well above, but its threads are separated below, so the Holy One—in a manner of speaking, the Soul of all souls—[created in such a way that] the souls of all Israel above are intertwined, but below each one has an individual soul. And it is for this reason that the people of Israel are called one nation.[8]

Now while this account does not explicitly express the concept of organic unity as delineated above, it comes sufficiently close to it. First, it emphasizes the unity of the Jewish people in

---

[7] Deuteronomy 32:9.
[8] *Hamek Davar* on Deuteronomy 32:9

the spiritual domain. In addition, the metaphor of the rope suggests that if a disturbance occurs in part of the rope, it is transmitted throughout its entire length, a character similar to the spreading of pain to the entire organism when one of its parts is infected.

Rabbi Joseph B. Soloveitchik also directed attention to the spiritual solidarity of the Jewish people, again in a transcendent sense, in an essay entitled "The Synagogue as an Institution and Idea." He wrote:

> When we pronounce the term *keneset yisrael*, we refer not only to a multitude consisting of thirteen million people, our contemporaries, *ken yirbu* but to a mystical entity or individuality. *Keneset yisrael*, the way Nahmanides, and other mystics, the classical *ba'ale ha-kabbalah*, understood the term, is not just a conglomeration of people. It is not just a crowd. It is more than that. It is a separate entity, a living individuality provided with an "I" awareness. The kabbalists spoke about the invisible *keneset yisrael*. There is a visible *keneset yisrael* which consists of contemporaries, of thirteen million people now. There is an invisible *keneset yisrael*, which embraces not only contemporaries, but every Jew who has ever lived.[9]

Rabbi Shlomo Goren, however, insisted that the concept of organic unity contained in the idea of *areivut* is not merely transcendental but also, in a meaningful sense, physical. To support his view, he cited a commentary in the Jerusalem Talmud on the verse "You shall not take revenge, you shall not exact retribution from among your people,"[10] which he interprets as implying a spiritual unity in the organic sense, as follows:

---

[9] In *The Rabbi Joseph H. Lookstein Memorial Volume*, ed. Leo Landman (New York: Ktav, 1980), p. 337.
[10] Leviticus 19:18.

> If someone is cutting meat and one hand cuts the other,
> does it make sense to suggest that the hand that was cut
> shall take revenge against the other by an act of retalia-
> tion? Such are the relations within the Jewish community.
> All Israel is like one body; it is therefore just that one shall
> not avenge himself against another because it is like
> revenging oneself against oneself.[11]

In sum, the organic view of Jewish unity can be interpreted as applicable to both the Jewish body and the Jewish soul; it has both physical and spiritual connotations. Physically it means that the pain of one Jew is the pain of all Jews. Spiritually it means, first, that every Jew is subject to punishment for sins committed by others which he could have prevented, and sec-ond, that every Jew has an obligation to influence his fellows to adhere to the religious precepts of Judaism—moral as well as ritual.

The moral implications of the organic view of the unity of the Jewish people are obvious and several. As already noted, revenge against another Jew responsible for my injury is irra-tional; by hurting another, I hurt myself. It is easy to forgive another for his moral transgressions because I must hold myself responsible for them. When someone is being pursued by an assailant who intends injury or murder, I have an oblig-ation to intervene, because I must see myself, too, as the target of the assailant's malevolent intentions. When I perceive anoth-er Jew in dire straits, I must assist him to emerge from the con-ditions which threaten his life, because his pain is also mine; and so on. There are many rules of interpersonal conduct that can be rationalized on the basis of the Jewish conception of the organic unity of the Jewish people.

---

[11] *Torat Hashabbat Vehamoed* (Jerusalem: Achava, 1982), pp. 202–3.

III

The principle of *areivut*, which requires intervention in the lives of others to prevent transgression, needs to be distinguished from the principle of *tochachah* (rebuking) with which it can easily be confused. It is important to note that the modalities of the two differ in a variety of ways. First, *areivut* is more extensive; it is relevant in many circumstances to which the principle that requires the rebuking of another has no application. The domain to which the latter principle is germane is circumscribed in the Talmud, and in several ways. One such limitation is that rebuking is appropriate only when it is welcomed; otherwise it is best to refrain.

> Rabbi Elu'u said in the name of Rabbi Elazar son of Rabbi Shimon: Just as a man is commanded to say that which will be heard, so is he commanded not to say that which will not be heard. Rabbi Abba said that it is an obligation, for it is written, "Do not rebuke a cynic, because he will hate you; rebuke a wise man and he will love you."[12]

Rashi adds, by way of identifying the biblical source for this limitation, "For it is written 'Rebuke, thou shalt rebuke'; [the verb rebuke is repeated to imply] rebuke one who will accept it from you." No such limitation exists for the principle of *areivut*.

Another restriction on the application of the principle of rebuke! If the target of the criticism will be humiliated in the process, it is better to refrain.

> How do we know that if a person sees another committing an ugly act, he is obligated to rebuke him? For it is written, "Rebuke, thou shalt rebuke." If he rebukes him and the latter resists, how do we know that he must

---

[12] Yevamot 65b.

rebuke him once more? Therefore it is written, "Thou shalt rebuke" [which means," do it again"]. I would think [that he must continue to rebuke even] if his face changes [he experiences humiliation]. Therefore it is written, "You shall not sin because of him."[13]

The principle of rebuke may very well require that the process be repeated many times, even to a point where the one who is directing attention to the transgression is assaulted or cursed by the recipient of his words, but he may not embarrass the transgressor.

According to Rabbi Tarfon and Rabbi Elazar ben Azariah, the enterprise of rebuking seems no longer to be applicable, because, according to Rabbi Tarfon, no one in this (i.e., his) generation will accept rebuke. Rabbi Elazar ben Azariah added the more significant observation, "I wonder if anyone in this generation knows how to rebuke."[14] One could fairly maintain that the obstacles to the fulfillment of this commandment that prevailed in ancient days exist equally today.

The implication of both these judgments is that, at least since the days of Rabbi Tarfon and Rabbi Elazar be Azariah, the obligation to rebuke has been regarded as in the category of those *mitzvot* in the Torah that lack the concrete circumstances in which they become mandatory and to which they can be applied. But in all the situations delineated above, *areivut* is both possible and desirable. The reason for this resides in another distinction between the two. Rebuking is essentially negative in orientation. The one engaging in rebuke must inform the sinner that he stands in violation of a halachic precept. According to Maimonides,

If one sees a fellow Jew who has sinned or who has gone on an evil way, it is an obligation to restore him to the

---

[13] Eiruchin 16b.
[14] Ibid.

path of righteousness and to tell him that he sins against himself with his evil deeds, for it is written, "Rebuke, thou shalt rebuke your friend."[15]

It is one thing to tell a person that he has sinned, that he is wicked, and that he should repent—the way of rebuke, and quite another to speak to him about the contents of Torah, to explain how and why it enriches life, and to urge upon him the relation with the Supreme Being that can be achieved by Torah living. It is because of the negativity of the method of rebuke that the sages described Moses as offering words of chastisement immediately before his death only in indirect, elliptical terms. On the initial verses in the book of Deuteronomy where Moses lists the locations included on the itinerary of the people of Israel as they traveled through the desert, Rashi writes:

> Because these are words of rebuke, and he [Moses] recounted all the locations where they caused anger before the Almighty, therefore he concealed what they did and merely hinted at them.

The result of emphasizing the positive and qualifying the negative is greater harmony and unity within the Jewish community. Our conclusion is not only that *areivut* and *tochachah* are different, but that *areivut* is, for the reasons here adumbrated, to be preferred. The practice of *areivut* may allow, but certainly does not require, rebuke. Its principal approaches consist of education, the application of the precept "Love your fellow Jew" even when he is a transgressor, and above all, presenting a model of commitment to Torah, a model which includes *ahavat yisrael*, the love of Israel that will inspire imitation and emulation.

---

[15] *Mishneh Torah*, Hilchot Deot 6:7.

Chapter 3

Justice and Mercy

Rabbinic sages recognized the difference between the moral rules implied by the ideal of justice (*mishpat*) and those that are an expression of the ideal of mercy (*chesed*). The fundamental moral precepts subsumed under justice were not, prior to the covenant at Sinai, *voluntarily* accepted but *imposed*. They were included among the Noachide commandments, specifically, the prohibition of stealing and murder, and the obligation to institute courts of justice in which civil and criminal cases can be adjudicated.[1] These precepts are deduced exegetically from a verse in the Bible whose essence is a command.[2] The moral precepts subsumed under mercy are not included among the Noachide laws and, according to rabbinic commentary, as noted above, were *voluntarily* accepted by the people of Israel

---

[1] The Talmud (Sanhedrin 57a) lists the seven Noachide precepts. One of these is *dinim*, which is interpreted by Maimonides as the imperative to establish courts of law to judge Noachides when they violate the seven precepts. According to Nachmanides (Genesis 34:13), *dinim* refers to many of the civil laws undertaken by the people of Israel at Sinai. On this view, the laws of justice imposed on Noachides are considerably more numerous.

[2] The phrase that introduces the Noachide commandments is "And God commanded the man." Cf. Sanhedrin 56b.

by covenant, even prior to Sinai, when they were enslaved in Egypt.[3]

The implication of this distinction is that the rules of justice have a mandatory basis irrespective of a voluntary gesture of covenantal acceptance, whereas those of mercy require such acceptance if they are to be obligatory. We may speculate as to the reason. Precepts of justice are introduced into society to adjudicate occasions of social conflict and prevent internecine strife, for otherwise chaos would reign supreme. Civilized society could not exist if it was not organized according to some rules of justice. The display of compassion and concern for others, normally inspired by some degree of commitment to the positive goal of enhancing human well-being, is not required by justice, which is focused on preventing violence rather than on social welfare. The precepts of mercy, on the other hand, direct attention to the need to introduce into human relations mutual concern and a common devotion of each to the other in order to create a community that is connected and cohesive. Compassion for the human existential condition is not a preoccupation of justice. Its objective is the management of social conflict.

Notwithstanding, the precepts of justice were also subsequently incorporated into the covenant voluntarily accepted by the people of Israel at Sinai. Accordingly, the Torah recognizes two bases for the obligations subsumed under the ideal of justice—one imposed and the other covenantal, that is, by means of a voluntary gesture of commitment.

I

We need to consider another implication of the covenantal character of the Jewish religion. In a society guided by

---

[3] *Yalkut Shimoni*, Deuteronomy 29:11.

covenantal commitments, moral precepts, that is, imperatives that obligate acts of both justice and mercy, are primarily interpreted, not in terms of *rights*, but in terms of *obligations*. Since every individual is mandated to fulfill the covenantal moral imperatives unconditionally, without anticipating a reciprocal gesture, it follows that one has no claim on the person one assists in the process of discharging a Torah imperative. For example, intervening in fulfillment of a biblical precept to save a person pursued by someone with malevolent intentions does not bring an entitlement to a reciprocal gesture: A's obligation to help B implies B's right to be helped, not A's right to be compensated by B.

An individual may evince a commitment to justice by dragging another to the courts to claim, in the name of justice, that his adversary should compensate him for, say, an injury he has sustained for which the other is responsible. Precepts of justice are utilized in this instance in the pursuit of self-interest. On the other hand, he may be upset by the injustice that prevails in society and the widespread pain it causes and may, in the name of justice, undertake initiatives to counteract it. His advocacy of justice is, in this instance, unselfish and altruistic. It is prompted by a sense of social responsibility and a concern for the well-being of others. It is inspired by his awareness of an obligation.

This is another crucial difference between a contractual and covenantal society. Rules of justice, in a contractual democratic society, will be regarded as primarily securing the rights of its members, while in a covenantal society, they will be perceived as principally enunciating obligations. For the Jew, even rules of justice demand selfless conduct. Each citizen has obligations to others to intervene in their behalf to ensure that justice is done. One may, of course, lodge a claim against another person in the name of justice, but this is not the primary function of justice, which is understood as imposing covenantal obligations.

II

In truth, rights and obligations are correlative, that is, wherever there are rights, there are obligations, and obligations are invariably associated with rights. If a citizen has the *right* of privacy, it follows logically that others have an *obligation* not to trespass on his property. If a man has an *obligation* to support his wife, it is a logical conclusion that his wife has a *right* to be supported.[4] Both rights and obligations are therefore available in a contractual as well as a covenantal society. The difference between the two is that a contractual society is rights-oriented; rights are assigned primacy, and the corresponding obligations flow from rights. The situation is in reverse in a covenantal society because it is obligation-oriented, that is, obligations are paramount. I have an obligation to pay a debt or to return a lost object to its owner. Each of these recipients has rights which flow from the primary biblical and rabbinic obligations.

Accordingly, the fundamental moral distinction, in the Jewish perspective, is not so much between acts of justice and acts of mercy, but between a covenantal perspective, in which acts of justice as well as mercy are required as a matter of categorical and unconditional obligation, and a contractual perspective, in which laws of justice are enacted to protect the

---

[4] Joel Feinberg argues in "The Nature and Value of Rights," *Journal of Value Inquiry* 4 (1970): 245–57, that there are obligations without correlative rights. He cites in support of this thesis the obligation to give charity even while no individual deprived of sustenance has a right to demand it. I argue below that in such circumstances the right belongs to the community. He also redefines "obligation" in terms of "requirement" rather than in terms of "duty to another" and suggests that the law may impose requirements without conferring rights. My view is that if the law requires action, there is some entity that can demand its performance, and that entity, whether community, state, or agency, has rights.

rights of citizens, and acts of mercy are perceived as voluntary and nonobligatory.

III

If, however, in the covenantal view, acts of both mercy and justice are fulfillments of obligations, and both are unconditional and therefore essentially unselfish, which means that the act of justice is itself, in the popular sense of the term, an act of mercy, what then is the difference between justice and mercy?

Note once again that rights and obligations are correlative. Therefore, if justice requires that A shall pay his debt to B, B has a right to *demand* payment. But can the same be said with regard to obligations to perform acts of mercy. In a covenantal society, A has an obligation to help the destitute and the afflicted in the form of charity. Does this mean that some B, an impoverished member of the community, has a right to *demand* from A a kind gesture? The answer is clearly negative; B may petition in his own behalf but cannot demand. Where then is the right that corresponds to the obligation? It is fair to say that the obligation is not directed toward any individual but to *society*; it is society that possesses the corresponding right. The individual recipient of generosity is, in this case, simply a means of fulfilling a citizen's obligation to society. Accordingly, in the covenantal view, while interpersonal justice directs attention to obligations that prevail among individuals,[5] interpersonal acts of mercy are at bottom obligations of individuals to society.

The *halachah* confirms this conclusion. It requires that everyone give charity, but it does not grant an individual the right to demand that he should be the person with respect to whom a

---

[5] I am not here discussing the variety of justice that a state metes out to its citizens, which is also social in character.

philanthropic act shall be fulfilled.[6] This is not to deny the existence of a personal, nonsocial psychological impetus to the performance of acts of mercy. An individual may be prompted by a feeling of sympathy or compassion to respond to someone in need. This clearly involves a person-to-person relationship. But such an act, rooted in compassion, is not a covenantal act; the latter requires that the act of mercy shall be performed out of commitment to the covenant.

IV

The concept of justice, in the covenantal perspective, requires further elucidation. Issues of justice arise in situations where persons have *claims* against each other. In what contexts do such claims arise? According to the contractual view, they occur when one person appropriates property belonging to another or fails to fulfill a material commitment in lieu of some good received from another. The introduction of a rule which requires that one person assist another when the latter encounters a situation where his life or material well-being is threatened is not a legal norm in a contractual society, because such conduct is normally perceived as an expression of mercy, not of justice. If someone intervenes to assist, his action cannot be interpreted as the fulfillment of an obligation but as a noble act of generosity.

In the covenantal view, on the other hand, the starting point is obligation. But there are two sources of obligation: (1) a personal commitment, as in the case of borrowing from a neighbor and promising to pay, and (2) a biblical or rabbinic command to perform with respect to another. Again, where an individual has a claim against another, which may derive from a personal commitment or a biblical imperative, the issue is not one of

---

[6] Yoreh Deah 248.

mercy but justice. Accordingly, the biblical precepts "Do not stand by as your brother's blood is shed" and "If you encounter the ox of your enemy or his donkey straying, you shall return it to him" are demands of justice. They are matters of justice because they imply a claim. The biblical imperative that I shall not remain indifferent to an attack launched upon another, but that I take steps to save him also refers to a total stranger whom I have never seen heretofore. The law requiring that I assist an individual whose animal has collapsed because it could no longer carry the burden on its back refers to a context where the animal's owner is my enemy at whose hands I may very well have sustained an injury. My obligations in both these instances are matters of justice even if my responses cannot be construed in terms of reciprocity. The reason is that in both such instances, the person I assist has a valid claim on me. The claim derives from a biblical command rather than from some obligation I may have undertaken in lieu of a favor received. But insofar as justice is concerned, it does not matter. The just claim need not be rooted in a benefit conferred; it may be a biblical imperative. What identifies a rule as one of justice rather than mercy is that a right exists corresponding to the obligation, and that the possessor of the right has a claim.[7]

---

[7] The possession of a claim does not necessarily mean that it is actionable and thus may be brought into a courtroom for adjudication. If one fails to assist a man whose animal is weighed down by an intolerable burden, one will not have to face litigation in the event that the failure to assist resulted in a loss to the animal's owner. Maimonides, in *Mishneh Torah*, Hilchot Rotzeach 13:2, states that the one who refrains from performing the obligation violates a negative and positive commandment and is subject to divine retribution. The implication is that he would not need to face sentence in a human court. Notwithstanding, the biblical precept that obligates a bystander to assist gives the owner a biblical right and claim, and is therefore a rule of justice.

Acts of mercy, on the other hand, are those for which no claim can be made on the part of the individual. Members of the covenantal community have an obligation to respond to the needs of the destitute and society, but no individual may *demand* of another an act of charity or hospitality. If, for example, a poor person appropriated the property of another on the grounds that he has a claim based on the right to receive charity, he would be treated as a thief. Even if the materially endowed individual set aside a certain sum for the purpose of discharging his philanthropic obligations, the poor person does not have the right to appropriate from that sum for himself without the donor's approval. The destitute do not have claims against individuals, and the distributions they receive from them are manifestations of mercy rather than justice. The choice as to who shall be the recipient of his philanthropic gestures, which are indeed obligatory, may be exercised by the donor himself. Such acts belong to the category of mercy.

IV

Accordingly, the principle of justice is relevant when individuals have *claims* against others, while the ideal of mercy comes into play when no such claims exist. Individuals may, however, *appeal* for assistance to others on the basis of their social obligation.

The individual's obligation to exhibit mercy does, however, imply a claim, for claims are based on rights, and rights and obligations are correlative. As noted above, it is the community, not an individual, which possesses the right corresponding to one's obligation to give charity. To that extent, a philanthropic act which is to be construed as an act of mercy on the part of the donor in relation to individuals is an act of justice in relation to the community. It is testimony to the fact that communities, unlike individuals, have a claim upon the charitable activities of their members, that historically communities exercised their right to institute a charity tax and to assess each member to a degree commensurate with his material substance.[8]

Accordingly, a member of the Jewish community could discharge his obligation to perform acts of charity in two ways—by choosing one or several persons who appeal for assistance, even though they do not have the right to demand it, to be the recipients of his largesse, or by contributing to institutions representing the community, which have the right to demand a charitable response.

We have determined that individuals cannot claim, though they may appeal for, acts of generosity from members of the community. Do they have a claim on the institutions designated for that purpose? It would appear that the answer is affirmative, and for the following reason. The individual has no obligation to perform an act of kindness in the interest of any specific person who is destitute; his obligation is to the community. The community's institutional agents, on the other hand, are mandated to perform such acts on behalf of individuals in need. This indeed is their *raison d'être*. There is, after all, a biblical obligation to provide for the poor. We may reasonably assume that these mandates obligate them to initiate programs of assistance for the afflicted and to respond to those whose need has been ascertained.

V

Rabbinic commentary asserts that God gave priority to *chesed*, acts of kindness, over *din*, acts of justice. The names of God, according to rabbinic interpretation, connote divine attributes. The name that appears in the first verse of the Bible,

---

[8] Cf. Yoreh Deah 248.

which declares that God created the heaven and the earth, is *Elo-him,* which according to rabbinic tradition refers to the Divine Being insofar as He guides the world in accordance with the attribute of justice. The name spelled *yud-hey-vuv-hey* and usually pronounced as *Ado-nai* refers to His attribute of mercy. The rabbis also noted that in an early verse of the second chapter of the Bible, in speaking of creation, God is referred to as *Ado-nai Elo-him,* that is, both names are used, by way of indicating that both attributes can be asserted of Him. But it is noteworthy that the one that expresses God's mercy is mentioned first, which prompts Rashi to comment:

> At first, God intended to create it [the world] to be ruled strictly according to the principle of justice, but He realized that the world could not thus endure; therefore He gave precedence to divine mercy and joined it with divine justice.[9]

It is clear that in God's application of retribution, mercy takes priority. Further, there is a well-known theological principle entitled *imitatio Dei,* which means that man has an obligation to imitate God. This principle receives the following elaboration in the Talmud: "As God is compassionate, so shall you be compassionate; as God is gracious, so shall you be gracious."[10] Apparently, the divine qualities we are urged to imitate are principally those of mercy. While justice remains an essential attribute of the Divine Being, the emphasis is on moral conduct derived from the ideal of mercy. Man is urged, in conformity with the requirement of the imitation of God, to give priority to the precepts of mercy.

Such priority occurs in three different contexts. There is (1) divine justice, (2) judicial justice, and (3) justice in interperson-

---

[9] On Genesis 1:1.
[10] Shabbat 133b.

al relations. The priority of mercy over justice in God's relation to man is expressed in the *shlosh esrei midot*, the thirteen attributes of mercy, which characterize the way the Divine Being relates to the human being. He is declared to be compassionate, gracious, long-suffering, abundant in mercy, and so on. He forgives easily and postpones punishment. The attribute of justice is not included among the thirteen. Further, if justice were more demanding, the sin would not as often be forgiven or the punishment so long delayed.

The priority of mercy in the judicial process is emphasized in the Talmud and the codes of Jewish law. There are two varieties of judicial justice: (1) the strict application of the law, and (2) compromise or arbitration, in which both litigants agree to submit to the decision of a court that will not necessarily decide the case in accordance with the strict requirements of justice. In these circumstances, it is possible that one of the litigants will be granted a material advantage, which, according to the strict application of the law, would constitute an injustice. The latter procedure is described as just nevertheless because each litigant understands that in agreeing to the arbitration procedure he surrenders his ownership of that which, according to the rigorous interpretation of the legal principle, belongs to him and, were it not for his concession, would be perceived as an injustice. Hence, the concession offered in the act of compromise or in the agreement to arbitration is, in effect, an act of mercy. Jewish law recommends this variety of justice, which includes a gesture of mercy, over the rigid application of the law.[11]

The third variety of justice is interpersonal. Normal relations among individuals, outside the realm of business affairs, are usually guided by considerations of mercy rather than justice. Issues that require adjudication generally result from conflicts, and such matters are best left to the courts, in which case they

---

[11] See Choshen Mishpat 12:2.

are instances of judicial justice. It is in this interpersonal context that the principle of the priority of mercy is most significant.

A major reason for the priority of mercy, and this should not be perceived as a derogation of the importance of justice, is that the consequences of the application of justice in human affairs are essentially preventive. Laws of justice are designed to eliminate conflict in the community. In many circumstances, they contribute to peace, which is essentially a state in which nations do *not* raise sword against nation, and wars are *not* fought. Acts of kindness, on the other hand, according to rabbinic judgment, are socially constructive in that they contribute to the creation of a connected and cohesive society. This is a principal objective of the employment of the instrumentality of the covenant in Jewish life. The covenant, which is the defining and most fundamental concept in terms of which Judaism is to be understood, is an instrument intended to coalesce the descendents of the patriarchs into a *people*. The biblical covenant was not primarily a means of defining interpersonal relations[12] but those between God and the *people* of Israel. In the Covenant-between-the-Parts, the land of Israel was given to the descendants of Abraham, that is, the people of Israel. Subsequently, the Sinaitic covenant, as well as the one in the fields of Moab and the other at the mountains of Gerizim and Eval, were instruments by which the *people* of Israel undertook obligations to live by the Torah. The communal nature of these undertakings, however, is manifest in the formula of acceptance that was uttered at Sinai, namely, "*we* shall perform, *we* shall obey," and especially in the rabbinic interpretation of the significance of the covenant drawn at the two mountains, which, they explained, was the means through which the people undertook to serve as guarantors for each other;[13] the latter covenant

---

[12] It was used for such a purpose as well. Cf. the covenants between Abraham and Avimelech, and Jacob and Laban.

[13] See Chapter 2 above on the role of the guarantor.

adding cohesion to the people of Israel. This biblical goal could not be accomplished by the universal application of the principle of justice but only by covenantal undertakings to engage in interpersonal relations according to the mandates of mercy. The preoccupation of Jewish covenantal theology with the task of creating a people in a manner that would ensure their connectedness and solidarity is a major reason for the priority of mercy over justice.

There are circumstances, it is true, in which it would appear that concern for the individual transcends that for the community. Rabbi Akiva taught that the biblical verse "Your brother shall live with you" means that your life takes precedence over your brother's. Further, if an enemy attacks a Jewish community and demands the surrender of one individual for death, and warns that if its demand is refused, the lives of all will be taken, the community is not permitted to acquiesce. These conclusions, however, are not relevant to the question of priority in the relation of justice and mercy and the issue of communal solidarity, but to the value of human life. For Judaism, its value is infinite; man was created in the image of the Infinite God and shares in His infinite value. The concept of infinity, as defined mathematically, means that the part is equal to the whole.[14]

---

[14] Bertrand Russell, in his book *Mysticism and Logic*, explained this concept by example. He noted that the set of natural numbers and the set of even numbers are equi-numerous. This can be demonstrated by exhibiting a one-to-one correspondence between the members of the two sets. Both sets are infinite even while the set of even numbers has half the members of the set of natural numbers. He therefore defined the concept of infinity (a definition introduced into mathematics by Georg Cantor) as that number in which a part is equal to the whole. This concept can be used to explain the halachic conception of the value of an individual human life. The value of the individual is equal to the value of the community, that is, the part is equal in value to the whole.

This definition is relevant here. The life of one person is equal in value to the value of the lives of all the members of a community.[15]

The halachic preoccupation with the welfare of the community is also expressed in the precept that an individual is not permitted to spend all his material goods on charity. He is obligated to retain a substantial portion for himself and his family. The reason is that by disposing of all his goods, no matter how generous and praiseworthy it may seem from the perspective of mercy, he is really turning himself and his family into a burden on the community,[16] and this is contrary to the requirements of mercy, whose principal function is to enhance well-being rather than to cause harm to the community.

The primary biblical focus in its assessment of the relative importance of the principles of justice and mercy, therefore, is the people of Israel. Consequently, an act of mercy, which contributes to the solidarity of the Jewish community, takes precedence over the implementation of justice among individuals.

This should not be taken to mean that individual human life is of ultimate value, and that there is nothing whose value exceeds that of man. If this were the case, a man's life could not be taken, no matter what the crime, under any circumstances. But Judaism recognizes the existence of an obligation to do so in certain cases. However, Cantor also demonstrated that there are different levels of mathematical infinity, some of a higher order than others. Such a concept is also applicable in assessing the infinite value of human life in relation to other values that possess higher levels of infinity.

[15] For a detailed exposition of this point, see the chapter entitled "Individualism" in my *Halakhah and Politics: The Jewish Idea of a State* (New York: Yeshiva University Press, 1988).

[16] Cf. Ketubot 50a. "It was enacted in Usha that, should he want to be liberal in philanthropy, he should not part with more than a fifth, for otherwise he would become a burden on society."

VI

It is frequently observed that for Judaism, acts of mercy are simultaneously acts of justice. It is noted that the word *tzedakah* which means "charity," is taken from the word *tzedek*, which means "righteousness." This judgment contains an element of truth, for the very act which is an expression of mercy vis-à-vis the individual is simultaneously a manifestation of justice in relation to the community.

Chapter 4

The Right and the Good

A crucial biblical imperative requiring moral conduct is *ve-useesah hayashar vehatov*, "you shall do the right and the good." Nachmanides notes that explicit and detailed laws of Torah already prescribe moral conduct. What then, he asks, is added by this generic imperative? He answers that it is not possible for the Torah to enunciate laws precisely descriptive and applicable to all moral situations that may arise, and thus a general principle is needed to provide guidance in circumstances covered by no explicit biblical law. This service is rendered by the principle requiring conduct that is right and good.[1]

Rabbi Aharon Lichtenstein argued that moral conduct, while not always obligated by *din*, explicit law, is nevertheless a requirement of *halachah*, which subsumes under its general rubric both that which is articulated in Torah[2] and that which

---

[1] Deuteronomy 6:18.
[2] The concept of Torah should be understood as including both the written and oral laws as well as those rabbinically commanded. It is obvious that rabbinic laws cannot, any more than the biblical, fully cover the entire gamut of human experience to which some moral rule is relevant.

is not.[3] Accordingly, *halachah* recognizes two kinds of sanction for moral conduct—obligations enunciated by explicit precepts of Torah, and those that may be deduced from the principle "You shall do the right and the good."

I

But how can we arrive at the principles concerning the right and the good if they are not enunciated? If divinely mandated rules are not available to provide guidance and instruction, by what criteria can we determine what is right and good?

Ethical rules of conduct, explicit or not, are in the category of the precepts that rabbinic literature refers to as *sichliot*, rational commandments. They are rational in the sense that if they had not been prescribed, mankind would inevitably have enacted them as laws to guide interpersonal relations. Such are, for example, "Thou shalt not kill" and "Thou shalt not steal." Precepts deduced from "the right and the good" may also be assumed to be rational. We may conclude, then, that there are two categories of rational precepts—those that are commanded and in addition are rationally compelling, and those arrived at by rational considerations alone.

But what is meant by reason and rationality in this context? Some regard moral law as inherent in the nature of things. The universe, they argue, is guided by both physical and moral laws, all of which can be ascertained by the faculty of reason. Another view has it that when the fetus emerges from the womb, it is already endowed with knowledge of fundamental moral precepts. This knowledge is regarded as consisting of self-evident propositions that prompt immediate assent. Moral precepts are accordingly innate, that is, they are already con-

---

[3] Cf. his essay "Does Jewish Tradition Recognize an Ethic Independent of Halakhah?" in Menachem M. Kellner, *Contemporary Jewish Ethics* (New York: Sanhedrin Press, 1978), pp. 102–23.

tained in the human mind at birth. Such a claim might lead to the conclusion that intuition is a source of moral obligation; but it is an intuition which may appropriately be designated as rational because it involves an immediate grasp of moral precepts lodged in the faculty of reason that are perceived as imposing obligations. Others speak of deducing moral precepts from a central principle, such as the Kantian categorical imperative, which is itself held to be innate and located in the faculty of practical reason. An alternative view defines the good in utilitarian terms, and maintains that moral precepts can be deduced from the goal of serving social or individual interests, taking into account the nature of man and society. Human beings, as a matter of fact, seek self-preservation and a good quality of life. These values, and the imperatives that derive from them, are perceived as rational because they are justified by the faculty of reason, which calculates individual or communal well-being. On each of these interpretations, moral rules may be regarded as rational.

Rabbinic scholars offer similar arguments to support the claim that moral rules are rational in essence. Saadia Gaon declares that moral principles are immediately self-evident. After enumerating a series of categories of commandments which he identifies as rational—and the rules of morality are clearly among them—he writes, "Now the approval of these classes of acts that we have been commanded to carry out *is implanted in our minds*."[4] But Saadia also acknowledges that they can be justified by utilitarian and consequential considerations, such as the need to diminish pain and to secure the survival and viability of the community, a divine objective.

Divine Wisdom imposed a restraint upon bloodshed among men, because if license were to prevail in this mat-

---

[4] Cf. *The Book of Beliefs and Opinions* (New Haven: Yale University Press, 1948), p. 140.

ter, they would cause each other to disappear. The consequence would be, in addition to the pain experienced by the victims, a frustration of the purpose that the All-Wise had in mind in regard to them.[5]

It can be argued that according to Saadia, utilitarian considerations are paramount. Even if moral rules were implanted in a child at birth, the divine reason for doing so is to ensure the well-being of individuals, that is, the elimination of sources of pain, and to achieve the divine intent of securing a viable population on earth. Maimonides appears also to utilize both bases to justify the conclusion that reason sanctions moral imperatives independently of their divine origin. He wrote, "Their reasons are evident, and their utility in this world is known."[6] It can be maintained, though it is not as clear, that he, like Saadia, combines both varieties of explanation to support the claim that moral precepts are rational.

This is also the thrust of those thinkers who engaged in the enterprise of supplying *taamei hamitzvot*, reasons for the commandments. When they rationalize the commandments, they do so by demonstrating that the *mitzvot* serve the interests of man and society, that is, that the commandments were prescribed because they are advantageous, in a biological, social, and spiritual way, to human development and well-being and to communal welfare.

There is another reason that justifies identifying as rational commandments that flow from the precept that commands action that is right and good. It can be argued that the nonexplicit precepts derived from "the right and the good" carry some relationship to those explicitly enunciated. An examination of the halachic imperatives in the latter category reveals that they are invariably applications of two ideals, namely, jus-

---

[5] Ibid., p. 141.
[6] Cf. *Mishneh Torah*, Hilchot Meilah 8:8.

tice and mercy. It may then be argued that any other moral imperatives incorporated in the Jewish system of morality must be consistent with these ideals. Hence, the supplementary precepts derived from "the right and the good" may be regarded as rational on two grounds—first, because they can be justified by utilitarian considerations, that is, their usefulness to man and society, and second, because of their consistency or coherence with the ideals of justice and mercy.

One may have the impression, since the verse enunciating the precept which requires conduct that is right and good reads "You shall do that which is right and that which is good *in the eyes of God*," that the rules that express the content of the right and good flow directly from the Divine Will. Such an interpretation, however, would be erroneous. That which is *implied* by the concept of the right and good is not formulated as explicit Torah obligations. Inevitably, the task of identifying the right and the good is left to man. If however he allows his conduct to be guided by reason, utilizing it to demonstrate utility and to exhibit coherence between the precepts that prescribe conduct that is right and the good and the twin biblical ideals, he is, in effect, doing that which is right and good in the eyes of God.

II

A violation of Torah laws constitutes *sin*, while a transgression of the nonmandated dictates of reason is identified as *evil*. The essence of sin is not that the perpetrated act was inherently wrong or was incompatible with social interests, although this may very well be the case, but that the action contradicted a divine command. The fact that it was commanded confers infinite value on its performance; its transgression constitutes a repudiation of the Divine Will, and the seriousness of the transgression is of corresponding magnitude. Every action performed in relation to others and in violation of a divine imperative is two-dimensional. It has a horizontal component, that is, the act is perceived as a violation of an obligation to another and as detrimental to individuals or society. More important in a theological perspective, however, is its vertical component, namely, it is a repudiation of a precept expressive of the will of God.[7] It is the second of these two aspects that is intended when such a transgression is identified as sin. A violation of a precept that is not explicitly mandated, on the other hand, is not a direct repudiation of the Divine Being but a rejection of a command of reason which is perceived as approved by the Divine Being. If one wants to identify it as sin, one can do so, but in only a derivative and secondary sense, for the principle "you shall do the right and the good" commands, in effect, that the individual should obey the voice of reason.

Accordingly, the violator of a moral precept of reason is not identified as a *chotei*, a sinner, but as a *rasha*, a scoundrel.[8] Here are some rabbinic illustrations. The Talmud declares that if a poor man is searching for food and finds it, and another comes along and appropriates it with a physical gesture that constitutes a legal act of acquisition which the poor man failed to perform, the food legally belongs to the one who snatched it, but he is called a *rasha*, a scoundrel.[9] This is clearly a case where the aggressor committed a moral violation—his transgression is rooted in the biblical principle demanding action in consonance with the right and the good—but it was a precept of reason that he violated, not a divine imperative.

If an individual fails to fulfill his duties as prescribed by reason, there may be other consequences in addition to his being

---

[7] Cf. Rashi in Sanhedrin 10a, s.v. *makos bemukom misah omedes.*

[8] This is not intended to suggest that a *chotei* (sinner) is never called a *rasha*. To the contrary! One who violates biblically prescribed *mitzvot* is explicitly referred to as a *rasha*. What is intended is that those who violate nonexplicit moral imperatives are in the category of *rasha* only.

[9] Kidushin 59a.

identified as a scoundrel, with the social ostracism this characterization may bring in its wake. In Jewish law, a legal act of acquisition must be performed to transfer title to an object. If, for example, A sells B a basket of fruit, an acceptable mode of acquisition is *hagba-ah*, that is, B picks up the basket. The transfer of money, on the other hand, is not a validating act of acquisition in the case of movable property. Now, if B purchases and pays for the fruit but has not yet performed the necessary title-appropriating act, the seller has a right to change his mind. Should he do so, however, he is subject to the following imprecation: "He who punished the people of the generation of the flood and the generation of the dispersion will also punish those who do not act upon their word."[10] In other words, the violator is not regarded as a sinner but as one who deserves an imprecation, that is, a *rasha* with punitive consequences.

There is another rule in this category, according to the talmudic sages, which even allows a *bet din* to use coercive tactics to compel an individual to comply. This method goes beyond calling an individual a *rasha* or even pronouncing an imprecation upon him. It would, in effect, allow the application of physical force. The rule in question is a prohibition of acting according to *midat sdom*, an abominable trait characteristic of the people of Sodom; it is a trait that prevents one from doing anything that would prove advantageous to another person even if one loses nothing in the process. A case in point is the distribution of the real property of a father's estate among a number of sons where one of them already has ownership of a piece of land adjoining the estate. The son with the property contiguous to the estate requests that when the estate is apportioned, his should be the section alongside the land he already owns. If his request is granted, all things other than location being equal, he will gain an advantage while the others lose

---

[10] Baba Metzia 44a.

nothing. The Talmud declares that his siblings should consent to his request, if there is no feature of the requested portion that renders it superior to the other portions. A failure to do so would brand the brothers as conducting themselves in the tradition of the sodomites. Should they persist in their refusal, the courts could intervene to coerce the result. When Nachmanides explains the meaning of "the right and the good," he refers to this case as an outstanding example.[11]

III

Notwithstanding the greater seriousness attached to the violation of an explicit command, the principle of utility sanctioned by reason plays a crucial role in *halachah* and, at times, is even assigned priority over a biblical precept. There are instances, in resolving matters of a fiscal nature, in which the *halachah* encourages the application of the utilitarian guideline, based on purely rational considerations, rather than the implementation of explicit precepts. There is a striking passage in the Talmud concerning a rabbinic edict allowing a husband to inherit the estate of a wife whom he married, with the approval of her brothers, when she was a minor. The marriage, arranged by her brothers because her father was deceased, has validity by rabbinic but not by biblical criteria. Notwithstanding, the rabbis decreed that the husband should inherit the wife's estate. They did this to prevent resentment by a husband toward his wife because he would be denied the right of inher-

---

[11] Cf. Baba Batra 12b. There is an argument between Rabba and R. Yosef as to what constitutes equal distribution, but both agree that *kofin al midas sdom*, the *bet din* compels one who conducts himself as a sodomite to do the right and the good. See also Baba Metzia 108a, which explicitly relates this example to the principle "you shall do what is right and what is good." See also Nachmanides' commentary on Deuteronomy 6:18.

itance granted to husbands whose marriages were biblically sanctioned. The Talmud then addresses this situation as follows:

> But by biblical standards, the father inherits her estate [meaning that the estate should pass through him, since he is deceased, to his descendants], and it is only rabbinically that the husband has a claim to the inheritance? [In other words, how can a rabbinic edict suspend the application of a biblical precept?] [The answer is] The *bet din* has the authority to deprive an individual of the ownership of his property.[12]

This response means that the biblical principle was not suspended but circumvented. The power granted to a *bet din* to nullify a person's title to property is a generic talmudic principle rather than one applicable exclusively to inheritance. In this instance, the rabbis did not formulate new rules of inheritance incompatible with biblical prescription; they merely removed the property from the father's possession and assigned it to the husband. They were able to do this because of the principle, biblically rooted, that *hefker bet din hefker*, that is, a rabbinic court has the power to deprive an individual of the ownership of his property. The superiority of the biblical principle is thereby acknowledged, but it is, nevertheless, set aside. Here is an outstanding example—outstanding because the principle which affirms the right of the rabbis to remove property held by an individual has application in many different contexts, thereby allowing circumvention in many other circumstances—in which the principle of rational utility functions by way of offering halachic resolutions of moral issues in ways that might be perceived as astonishing.

---

[12] Yevamot, p. 89b.

The principle requiring that we do "the right and the good" is also relevant to the halachic rule that requires the subordination of the ideal of justice in the interests of the application of mercy. This rule is implicit in the talmudic discussion of two varieties of justice—one is the application of the law, and the other, the use of arbitration in which the law is compromised.[13] The code of Jewish law gives priority to arbitration, notwithstanding that Jewish civil law will not be strictly applied.[14] In such a case, preference is granted to considerations of utility over explicit commands, because even if the results of arbitration do not correspond to what is required by explicit law, litigants who present conflicting monetary claims are permitted to agree, prior to judgment, that they are willing to forgo what objectively belongs to them in the interest of arriving at an amicable conclusion (they are, in effect, renouncing ownership, in advance, of a portion of their property to accord with the judicial decision). The litigants here are guided by utilitarian considerations. It should also be noted that arbitration (*pshara*) is cited by Nachmanides and Rashi as an example of the application of the principle of the right and the good.

Here is an example of the use of the concept of the right and the good to resolve a matter that requires the application of justice. There is a talmudic principle which may be called the principle of fairness. In talmudic parlance, it is expressed in the phrase *god o agod,* which may be explained by example. When it is necessary to divide property between partners in circumstances in which a physical separation of the object into two portions is not feasible, perhaps because of smallness of size, one of them may propose a formula and suggest *god o agod.* He declares: I am willing to buy your share of the object at a cer-

---

[13] This distinction is discussed earlier in this volume.
[14] Choshen Mishpat 12:2.

tain price or to sell my share to you at the same price.[15] Other talmudic commentaries interpret this proposal as meaning that before its presentation, the property was assessed to determine its objective market value, and the offer utilized this value as a basis for the presentation.[16] On either interpretation, it ensures that the one who makes the proposal is sensitive to the importance of an equitable distribution. It should be noted that this arrangement may be regarded as fair because it results from the perception that the interests of each party to the arrangement will be equally served. It conforms to a utilitarian standard.

IV

The meaning of utility in Jewish thought differs significantly from the sense assigned to it in general philosophic discourse. The secular utilitarian thinker, as understood by John Stuart Mill, for example, is a hedonist; he is one who has adopted pleasure as the ethical ideal. Human happiness is his goal, and for him happiness means pleasure. The laws of society are to be regarded as moral if they serve communal self-interest, and they do so if they maximize pleasure for the community. Judaism rejects the notion that pleasure is worthy of adoption as the goal of life. Saadia, in the passage quoted above, did make the observation that the moral precepts of Judaism are rational for several reasons, one of which is that they contribute to the reduction of pain. But the recognition of the value of reducing pain is not to be translated into a justification of the pursuit of pleasure as life's goal. The experience of pain could

---

[15] Choshen Mishpat 171; Maimonides, *Mishneh Torah*, Hilchot Shecheinim 1:2, offers another interpretation that also reflects the principle of fairness.
[16] Cf. Meiri on Baba Batra 13a.

interfere with a concentrated effort to achieve any religiously sanctioned goal of human life.

If pleasure were the Jewish ethical ideal, as it generally is for those who advocate the philosophic doctrine of utilitarianism, pain could not be regarded as possessing either inherent or instrumental value. It is true that the hedonist will grant that pain is at times inevitable, in the sense that by the application of a painful process, surgery for example, a large quantity of pleasure could result, and it would be a rational decision to submit to it. However, he would regard it as preferable if the surgery were to be performed without pain. The involvement of pain in human welfare is thus essentially in the category of a necessary evil. The single-minded focus of the hedonist remains the accumulation of pleasure. But for Judaism, the value of the experience of pain is entirely unrelated to pleasure. Its importance, according to one biblical account, is pedagogical; it shapes character and contributes to the appreciation of Torah values.

> He [God] subjected you to hardships and hunger and gave you manna to eat, which neither you nor your fathers have ever known, in order to teach you that man does not live by bread alone, but that man may live on what the Lord decrees.[17]

It is an experience of positive, although instrumental, value; it educates and humanizes.

The Talmud also distinguishes between two categories of pain. One of these is designated *yesurin shel ahavah,* pain that is inflicted by the Almighty because of love, that is, pain whose value resides in the shaping of personality and inspiring a closer relation with God.[18] The other variety of pain is severe and

---

[17] Deuteronomy 8:3.
[18] See the discussion in Berachot 5a.

intolerable and serves no constructive human purpose. Clearly, when pain is intense, it in effect paralyzes the individual, renders him incapable of responding to obligations, and prevents him from leading a constructive life for himself, his family, and his community. This is the meaning of Saadia's declaration; the application of moral precepts in interpersonal behavior is intended to reduce pain to allow individuals to preserve the capacity to live creatively. The pursuit of pleasure, then, is not, in the Jewish perspective, an ethical goal; it is not what the Jewish utilitarian doctrine is all about.

Jewish utilitarianism seeks the experience of satisfaction for its adherents, but the form that it advocates is not pleasure but joy. Satisfaction can take several forms—one is the satisfaction associated with the removal of pain, another with the experience of pleasure, and a third with the sense of joy. Judaism's emphasis is on joy rather than pleasure. Pleasure is experienced in isolation—a human being eating a hearty meal with no one around his table experiences pleasure; joy is rooted in relationships. Marriage brings joy to the couple embracing a new relationship. The service of God, for the deeply religious individual, results in a supreme variety of joy. Further, pleasure is experienced when the satisfaction is a concomitant of receiving—the person enjoying a steak in isolation cannot be perceived as giving of himself; joy accompanies the experience of giving. A human being will not do anything that is bereft of all satisfactions, but he can acquire it from activities that produce pleasures or from those that are motivated by love and dedication which inspire giving and sharing, experiences that result in joy. There is, after all, joy in giving. Judaism seeks to cultivate the spirit of altruism among its adherents because it is a religion of obligation and understandably strives to instill among its followers the satisfaction of giving. More on this later!

Indeed, it may fairly be said that in the perspective of Judaism, the ethical ideal for the human being is happiness, but happiness is defined, unlike the view of hedonism, as joy rather than pleasure. It is the aim of Jewish life to mould the character of those identifying with it to experience the most intense satisfaction, not in stimulating the senses but in responsibility expressed in relationships that inspire unselfishness.

Chapter 5

Rationality

Rationality consists of two components—one intellectual; the other ethical. Classically, Jewish thinkers interpreted its intellectual component as the view that one can, by contemplating the contents of one's own mind, arrive at truths about the universe.[1] Maimonides belongs to this category of thinkers. He begins the second part of his great philosophic work with a recitation of "twenty-five of the propositions that are employed in the proof for the existence of God."[2] These propositions are products of pure thought. Consider by way of illustration the first two of these premises. (1) The existence of an infinite magnitude is *impossible*. (2)The co-existence of an infinite number of finite magnitudes is *impossible*. The method of exhibiting the truth of such propositions can only be rational, not empirical; for *impossibility* is not subject to empirical verification. Maimonides was clearly a rationalist in the intellectual sense.

But Maimonides was also a rationalist in the ethical sense. An ethical rationalist is someone who (1) adopts a specific goal which he perceives as essential for a meaningful life, (2) utilizes

---

[1] See above, Chapter 4.
[2] *The Guide of the Perplexed*, trans. M. Friedlander (New York: Hebrew Publishing Co., 1881), pt. II, pp. 1–11.

reason to determine the actions that are conduits to the realization of that goal, and (3) exerts himself to ensure that emotions
will submit to reason in arriving at decisions. Human beings
have a variety of dispositions and in varying degrees, prodding
them in directions that are both contradictory and inimical to
their well-being. The rational individual adopts the guidelines
that reason identifies as flowing from the goal he has chosen
and strives to conduct his life in conformity with them.
Maimonides writes:

> What is the corrective for those who are sick in soul? They
> should go to the wise who are physicians of the soul, and
> they will heal their maladies by instructing them in the
> dispositions they should acquire till they are restored to
> the right path. Of those who realize that their dispositions
> are bad and nevertheless do not resort to the wise to be
> cured, Solomon says, "Wisdom and discipline, fools despise
> [emphasis added]."[3]

The first requirement is wisdom, which is essential for the
identification of the goal that will render life meaningful, but
equally important is discipline. Human dispositions need to be
taken into account, and they are emotional in essence. When
offering examples of dispositions, Maimonides cites anger,
arrogance, lust, greed, stinginess, generosity, cruelty, mercy,
and so on. These are emotions which require guidance and control to ensure that a person's actions will exemplify values consistent with the goal he has selected. Those who are ethically
rational, as Maimonides put it, utilize both wisdom and discipline.

It could be argued that the ethical component of rationality
is the more important. The requirement of intellectual rationality in Jewish religious life is generally regarded as desirable but

---

[3] Ibid., p. 54.

not mandatory. It is not necessary, for example, to prove the existence of God on the basis of true premises somehow written into the mind. If one does not accept such proofs and affirms His existence exclusively on the basis of belief, one is not, according to most Jewish thinkers, suffering from a deficiency in religious commitment, and for some this holds even if the beliefs one adopts deviate from the truth.[4] On the other hand, rationality in the ethical sense enjoys almost universal adoption; no one challenges Maimonides' insistence on the need for wisdom and discipline, that is, on the need for ethical rationality.

I

Rationality in the moral sense involves, as already noted, the selection of goals that give meaning to life. The selection requires wisdom. The choice of goals cannot be made on the basis of intellectual considerations alone. There are three human traits, often cited in conjunction, which are perceived to be indispensable to a successful life—*chachmah, binah, daat. Daat* is knowledge, an accumulation of facts, an awareness of realities, whose formulations can be included among the premises of a moral argument. *Binah* refers to the ability to utilize logic in arguments, to arrive by inference from premises to valid conclusions. The most important premises of a moral argument, however, derive from *chachmah*, wisdom, which consists in choosing a goal and its implied values that will render life

---

[4] We refer once again to the dispute between Maimonides and Rabbi Abraham Ibn Daud with regard to the erroneous acceptance of a false belief by a Jew. Maimonides labels such an individual a heretic, whereas Rabbi Abraham Ibn Daud argues that while the belief may be false, the Jew who entertains it preserves his religious credentials if his belief in God and his acceptance of Torah are not affected. Hilchot Teshuvah 3:7.

meaningful. Of course, the application of *chachmah* requires the employment of the purely intellectual faculties of *daat* and *binah*. *Chachmah* needs knowledge and logical inference, not for the purpose of justifying the chosen ultimate purpose, but to determine how the values it implies may be inferred from the ultimate goal, and how these values may best be achieved. But *chachmah*'s main focus, its essential characteristic, is the choice of the ultimate goal. Many who have accumulated an abundance of information and have a high I.Q. find, notwithstanding the great successes they may have attained, that they are essentially unhappy because of their unwise choice of values which are reflections of the essentially frustrating purposes they have selected as their goals in life.

There are many goals that present themselves as worthy of human consideration—pleasure, doing one's duty, a life devoted to intellectual achievement, responding to the will of God. One cannot, on the basis of *daat* and *binah*—that is to say, of a formulation of what are perceived as facts and the capacity to deduce conclusions by way of logical inference—give reasons or cite arguments why one of these should be preferred above the others. It is known that values cannot be deduced from facts. The end, the ultimate purpose of life, must first be chosen on the basis of some consideration other than *daat* and *binah*, and then these purely intellectual functions can be utilized to identify the values that flow from it and the means to achieve them. Judaism maintains that the ultimate purpose should be one which grants maximum meaning to human life. The right choice of such a purpose is an act of wisdom.

But ethical rationality requires not only the choice of a purpose; it also contains as an essential component the individual's exercise of control to overcome the enticing allure of objects that excite emotions and to ensure the realization of the values the chosen goal prescribes. This component of rationality is more difficult than its intellectual counterpart. Jews, for example, have a proclivity for intellectual activity. The Jewish com-

munity has often been referred to as an intellectual establishment. This means that Jews have *daat*, knowledge, and *binah*,
understanding. It is not at all clear that Jews are also blessed
with ethical rationality in impressive proportions. Statistically
speaking, their effort to set boundaries to action spurred by
emotion for the sake of the realization of value has not been
spectacular.

There is a fundamental difference between the intellectual
and the ethical. The former is geared to comprehension; the latter to action. The central concept of Judaism is not the principle
of faith, which requires essentially a theoretical response, that
is, intellectual appropriation of doctrine and an affirmation, but
the *mitzvah*, which prescribes conduct in accord with Torah values. The priority of the ethical, whose focus is action, to the
intellectual is accordingly implied. Judaism does advocate
rationality in the intellectual sense, but even more so, in the
ethical sense. Rabbinic literature distinguishes the *chacham*
from the *pikeach*. The latter is the one who possesses intellectual virtues but fails in the selection of the right values and falls
short in the exercise of willpower. Speaking of Korach, who ini-
tiated a rebellion against Moses, Rashi asks: How was it that
Korach, who was a *pikeach* (intellectually accomplished),
undertook this *shtut* (act of folly)? It is not sufficient to be
smart; what is needed above all is the utilization of our intellectual endowments in the service of the rigorous pursuit of
aims leading to a meaningful life.

Rationality in the ethical sense, therefore, consists in the
selection of a purpose and the values it implies, which have the
potential to suffuse life with meaning, and in the successful
resolve to live in conformity with them.

II

The factor that, more than any other, is recognized by
Judaism as productive of meaningful living and therefore enti-

tled to be adopted as the ultimate purpose is *commitment to transcendent values and eternal ideals*. Commitment is indispensable to the achievement of the goal. It consists of a powerful motivation to expend energy, wealth, and even life for the sake of another human being or a cause to which one attaches great value. The Torah puts it plainly. "Behold, I present you this day with a blessing and a curse; the blessing that you will listen to the commandments of the Lord your God." Listening means not only hearing and understanding, but also accepting—that is, committing oneself. It demands an expression of unselfishness and altruistic resolve. If one displays what appears to be unselfish generosity out of considerations of self-interest, one's attitude is interpreted as pragmatic, not as committed.

Commitment needs to be directed, if life is to have meaning, to transcendent values. A human being's life on earth is limited in quantity and achievement. The discovery of a new law or the formulation of a new theory of science, hailed as an extraordinary accomplishment, may be beyond dispute for only a relatively brief period, consisting of decades or perhaps centuries, and then repudiated as erroneous. The meaning of the life of Sir Isaac Newton or Dr. Albert Einstein does not, therefore, consist so much in the specific theories they introduced into the realm of science as in their devotion to the pursuit of truth, an eternal ideal. This is also the basis on which the worth of scientific lives of lesser stature is judged. The same holds for other ideals—justice, freedom, integrity, piety. Religious Jews who adhere conscientiously to the precepts of Torah because they recognize them as expressions of ideals, treasured in the human community, whose source is the Supreme Being find that their lives are most meaningful. Their source of meaningfulness is dedication to eternal values.

What is significant about commitment, in the first place, is that it is an indispensable prerequisite to genuine relationship. If you are committed, you are dedicated to someone or something, and this means that you are engaged in a relationship.

But relationships can be self-serving or selfless. If self-serving, they are temporary and superficial; they can easily be severed. They are, in effect, relationships without attachments. As soon as a person involved in such a relationship notices that it is no longer to his advantage to maintain it, it is dissolved. Relations rooted in dedication are lasting because they are essentially unselfish. They can form attachments stronger than those which join physical objects. Further, relationships may be of the celestial variety (i.e., relation with the Divine Being or Torah) or terrestrial in nature (i.e., relations within the human community), but all relationships of commitment contribute to a meaningful life.

It is necessary to counter a possible objection. In truth, life is also experienced as meaningful when it is creative, not only when it is committed. But can creativity alone render human life worthwhile; is creativity without commitment quite sufficient?

There is no doubt that creativity contributes significantly to personal satisfaction. It does so for a variety of reasons. The creative individual possesses a sense of human dignity. He is aware that through his creativity, he demonstrates his distinctiveness as a member of the human community. Animals can construct nests and lairs and care for their young, but they do so instinctively; they do not contemplate a purpose and institute a process designed to achieve it. It has been argued that even if a man's goal is the experience of pleasure, he still prefers pleasures that are distinctively human, namely, the pleasures of art, literature, and music. The reason for assigning priority to these pleasures, so the argument goes, is that they instill within the human being a sense of dignity.[5] This sense is stronger when the individual is not merely a spectator but a creator of artistic masterpieces. It is strongest when the person

---

[5] John Stuart Mill, *Utilitarianism* (New York: Liberal Arts Press, 1953).

engaged in creative activities of all kinds recognizes that in doing so he manifests the image of God.

In addition, the creative individual experiences a sense of power. His ability to transform stones and sand into palaces and scientific knowledge into technology instills within him a feeling of control over his life and the fate of his community. The feeling of distinctiveness in virtue of the fact that he possesses a creative capacity, a sense of power that manifests itself in the ability to exercise control, and an awareness that he is consequently a being possessed of dignity often combine to imbue man with the sense of self-worth necessary for a meaningful life. But is it quite sufficient?

The problem with creativity unaccompanied by dedication to human values and eternal ideals is that one can exhibit human distinctiveness by utilizing one's intelligence to build instruments of torture and annihilation. In doing so, one experiences no less a sense of creativity and a feeling of control over individuals and nations. Is the life of such an individual invested with meaning? Those who are preoccupied with the pursuit of ego satisfactions may offer an affirmative reply. Others, who take moral and spiritual values seriously, will introduce qualifications. The creators of the atomic bomb had serious misgivings. They recognized their power but questioned the value of their spectacular achievement because of the probability of its use in the service of death and destruction. The value of such products and the meaningfulness of the lives responsible for them can especially be challenged when mechanical inventions are explicitly undertaken, as the Nazis did, for diabolical purposes. These considerations lead to the conclusion that creativity without commitment to values that are humane does not lead to a life that is objectively recognized as meaningful. Some may find it satisfying, for their immediate murderous goals are achieved, and they may celebrate, but in truth their lives, even in their own perceptions, may not possess value. Those who undertake the destruction of human beings as an enterprise express a feeling of contempt for human life, *including their own*, that detracts from their sense of self-worth. Those who see themselves as beings of infinite value because of their spiritual character inevitably display reverence for all human life. Creativity, to be truly meaningful, must be a concomitant of unselfish commitment to both God and man.

It can be argued that a human being will never do anything unless it yields some kind of satisfaction. If this is true, and there is no reason to suppose it is not, may we not conclude that even the life of commitment is motivated by pleasure, and that it is pleasure rather than an identification with that which is of eternal value that is ultimately the central feature of a meaningful life? This inference is not valid, for human beings have the capacity to experience two kinds of satisfaction. One of these is based on receiving, on obtaining objects that serve their self-interest, that fulfill physiological and psychological needs. The other is based on giving, on the gratification gained by serving the needs of a beloved or a cause that one judges to be of extraordinary value. The satisfaction experienced when receiving a desired object is called pleasure; that felt when giving to an individual, to a community, to the Divine Being, or to a cause to which one is committed is labeled joy. In the Jewish perspective, joy is of greater value than pleasure precisely because it is a concomitant of a meaningful life. Joy, not pleasure, is a major objective of Jewish living. Satisfaction associated with commitment to God, which renders life supremely meaningful, is supremely joyful. But more of this later.[6]

Commitment to eternal values is a prerequisite to a meaningful life for still another reason, namely, it dispels loneliness. Loneliness is not overcome by the presence of a multitude, but by the development of relationships of a selfless variety. That the well-being of man depends on life in relationship rather than in isolation is the biblical assessment of the human condi-

---

[6] See below, Chapter 8.

tion. "It is not good for man to dwell alone" does not mean that man needs another, or many of them, to make his life more comfortable, but that he is dependent for his well-being on the presence of another, an object of love, to whose welfare he can also devote himself. A human being dwells alone in a congested city if he is deprived of genuine relationships. Transcendental commitment is undertaken by those who, inspired by religious faith and feeling, seek relation with God, a relation that brings with it supreme joy. But there are other relationships indispensable to human well-being—within a family, with teachers, and with the community. These relations need to be motivated by unselfish considerations, and all of them provide opportunities for that variety of satisfaction which is constitutive of joy and relieves loneliness.

Loneliness takes several forms. The focus of this discussion is its existential variety—the experience rooted in a human being's awareness that he is finite and that his life is of limited duration.[7] In this regard, he is totally helpless; it may be possible to extend his life span, but he cannot render it permanent. This consciousness generates anxiety and even depression, the essence of loneliness. His terrestrial life cannot be augmented, but it can be enhanced and the sense of loneliness relieved. This is achieved by identifying himself and, in effect, merging spiritually with other human beings, with the Divine Being, and with causes that embody eternal values. Rabbi Akiva was

---

[7] For Rabbi Joseph B. Soloveitchik in *The Lonely Man of Faith*, loneliness is a central theological category. His focus in this work is on the loneliness experienced by the man of faith, first, because of his sense of alienation when confronting the culture that surrounds him (sec. I A) and second, when he experiences himself as deprived of roots as a result of his restless and inevitable movements between what Rabbi Soloveitchik calls the natural and the covenantal communities (IX C). My concern here is the loneliness that is endemic to the human condition.

about to be burned at the stake, but he expressed gratification that he now had the opportunity to fulfill the commandment to love God even when his life was being taken from him. Rabbi Akiva was not lonely, though in the solitary condition of his cell awaiting execution, he may have experienced himself to be physically alone. The knowledge that a person's life can extend beyond his body and that he is not afflicted with its limitations brings relief to anxiety. In addition, the feeling of identification with eternal values brings with it a sense of joy.

Unselfish relationships dissipate loneliness because they expand life. If my relation with others is rooted in the knowledge that I will be the beneficiary of certain advantages because of it, then the focus of my life is exclusively myself. In addition, the relationship will last as long as I perceive myself to be a beneficiary. Should I discover that this is no longer the case, the relationship will end. If, on the other hand, the relationship is a manifestation of commitment, and my interest in another and devotion to him equals or transcends my concern with my own well-being, then that other—a friend or a spouse—is absorbed into myself, and my life is expanded and enlarged. A relationship of commitment, if mutually expressed, transforms different and discrete entities into a unity.

But it is not only unselfish relationship with people that counteracts loneliness; this will also be a consequence, but even more so, of commitment to causes that embody values. When an individual recognizes that something of enormous worth justifies some degree of sacrifice, and is prepared to expend of his substance and energies in its behalf, he in effect absorbs that cause into his own life, which is consequently united with it and enriched by it. He does not then experience, certainly not to the same extent as one who is incapable of commitment, the awareness and distress of being existentially alone. One who experiences no values that require unselfish commitment and is therefore incapable of truly devoting himself to family, community, and the Divine Being, because he lives for himself alone, is lonely even if he is surrounded by a multitude and immersed in endless pleasure-producing activities, because he cannot avoid the inevitable anxiety resulting from his own finitude.

The experience of loneliness, then, is not identical to that of being alone. Being alone is essentially a physical state of affairs, when, for example, an individual finds himself, at least for awhile, deprived of companionship. An individual in isolation but committed, on the other hand, is not lonely because of his identity with things whose value is permanent and even eternal. Especially is such loneliness largely, if not entirely, dissipated if he experiences unselfish attachments to the Divine Being.

Commitment, at least in the Jewish sense, is a prerequisite to a meaningful life for still another reason. It is productive of a sense of optimism that renders life palatable, and even joyful, in conditions of hardship and pain. Few people live in the real world. What we really see is an existing world edited by the attitudes we bring to the task of perception. The world we experience is structured, not only by the categories of our thought, but also by attitudes instilled by our beliefs and prescribed by our emotions. The imagination recreates reality to produce in our mind's eye a world that is consistent with our hopes or anxieties. The same world will look different depending on whether hope dominates (the optimistic view) or fear dominates (the view of pessimism). The optimist lives in a more satisfying world than the pessimist. Religious commitment, certainly of the Jewish variety, supports the sense of optimism.

This is not necessarily the case with commitment of a secular nature, which is typically replete with pessimism. One may be dedicated to, and even be willing to sacrifice in behalf of, the ideals of truth, justice, and peace without believing that they will inevitably be realized in human life on earth. Here is the testimony of one secular thinker:

Let us admit that, in the world we know, there are many things that would be better otherwise, and that the ideals to which we do and must adhere are not realized in the realm of matter. Let us preserve our respect for truth, for beauty, for the ideal of perfection which life does not permit us to attain, though none of these things meet with the approval of the unconscious universe. . . . To abandon the struggle for private happiness, to expel all eagerness of temporary desire, to burn with passion for eternal things—this is emancipation, and this is the free man's worship.[8]

For this secular thinker, human ideals are invented, not imposed; they are subjective, not objective; they are the products of the creative human imagination, but are nevertheless deserving of self-sacrificing commitment. Pessimism is normally a concomitant of such commitment. It is the commitment of the religious thinker, because of the addition of the element of faith, which can lead to a spirit of optimism that translates into confidence that the eternal values that mankind treasures will ultimately be achieved.

The result of pessimism is paralysis. An individual who believes that it is hopeless to strive for an unachievable goal will normally not struggle to attain it; notwithstanding the exceptions exemplified in the declaration of the atheist cited above. The implication is that a better community and a more satisfying world are created by those who are driven by the mood of optimism rather than by pessimism.

This is not to say that all religions instill optimism and inspire initiative among their adherents. A religion that teaches the doctrine of predestination and consequently supports the fatalistic view that all that happens in the life of an individ-

---

[8] From "A Free Man's Worship" in Bertrand Russell, *Mysticism and Logic* (Doubleday: New York, 1917), pp. 44–54.

ual is determined from the moment of birth will not encourage initiative. It will teach that it does not lie in the power of man to affect any kind of change, large or small, and its adherents, in all likelihood, will not venture into trailblazing paths. Further, a religion that relates its optimistic conclusions to life in the celestial world, and is pessimistic with regard to the world here and now, will also not normally engage in an attempt to transform it. It is a religion that teaches that human history will end with redemption, an optimistic view, and that man is free and competent to achieve it that has the power to inspire the human being to utilize his capacities and talents to produce a better world. This indeed is the Jewish view.

III

The second component of moral rationalism consists of the person's exercise of control over his emotions, so that what he does is consistent with the values to which he is committed. Are humans capable of responding to this challenge?

According to one theory, it requires an emotion of superior strength to overcome another emotion that is inferior, but pure reason, it is argued, which is intellectual in nature and devoid of emotion, can exert no influence over emotions. Such a conclusion is asserted in the context of a theory of determinism which claims that every action of a human being is the inevitable resultant of forces in the form of emotions that conflict with each other. The situation with regard to human action is perceived as entirely parallel to the movement of a ship at sea. The vessel is buffeted by opposing forces pushing in diverse directions, but the course it will take is ultimately that which physics calls the resultant, a velocity and direction that can be calculated in accordance with a precise formula. Analogously, it is argued, man is prodded by conflicting emotions, and the choice he will eventually make can also be interpreted, in a literal sense, as a resultant of emotional forces.

The Torah, the Talmud, and, with some exceptions,[9] Jewish philosophers rejected this conclusion if it is intended as a universal principle applicable to every instance of human conduct; man is perceived, rather, as endowed with power to exercise control over his life. It is useful, at this juncture, to distinguish between *will* and *desire*. The human organism is moved, as a result of an awareness of given circumstances, to experience a variety of different feelings. A beautiful object may excite appreciation or love. An insult may induce anger or even hatred. The sight of a suffering man may inspire pity or compassion. These emotions translate into *desires* to possess, to retaliate, and to share. Emotions can also be elicited by values just as they are by natural circumstances, that is, immediately and spontaneously. The sight of an individual in pain may prompt a charitable response, emotional in character, not only because of the feeling of compassion at the sight of suffering but also because of love for *mitzvot*, among which, of course, is the precept mandating assistance to the afflicted. The prophet Micah speaks of *ahavat chesed*, the love of kindness.[10] This refers, not to sympathy for the indigent, but to the love of a value that translates into desire. But actions also flow from nonemotional but theoretical commitment to values. One may, notwithstanding insensitivity to those afflicted, and simply as a matter of *obligation* imposed by a biblical precept that expresses a value, decide to contribute. Such a response is rational and a manifestation of will.

------

[9] Hasdai Crescas, the medieval philosopher and rabbi of communities in Aragon, Spain, was among them. According to Julius Guttmann in *Philosophies of Judaism* (New York: Holt, Rinehart & Winston, 1964), pp. 238–39, the determinism adopted by Crescas was not based on the argument of God's foreknowledge but on the workings of causality. It is the latter issue that provides the impetus for the contemporary debate concerning free will vs. determinism.

[10] Micah 6:8.

Desire, which results in a spontaneous reaction both to natural circumstances and to values, is either present or not, but if it is, it translates into an immediate visceral response. Thought is not an important factor in the process. If driven by conflicting emotions, we may contemplate the options, but when we finally act, the result, if it is an outcome of desire, is an inevitable consequence of the emotional forces that press upon us. The act of will, on the other hand, requires, as a prerequisite and as part of the process that results in action, the theoretical consideration of a value. If someone injures me, I may restrain anger, and recognizing the importance of refraining from hatred and retaliation, proceed on a course rationally illuminated by precepts of value leading to constructive relations.

We may put this distinction another way. On the level of the emotions, the feeling generated and the action that follows are in the nature of a *reaction*, similar to a reflex. A person who lives exclusively in the emotional realm has no freedom; all his actions are the resultants of emotional forces. When a person intervenes in circumstances in which he confronts a value that imposes an obligation and, simultaneously, a powerful emotion incompatible with the value, and he chooses the principle over the feeling, his action results from a *decision* rather than a reaction. In a decision, the rational consideration of a value is uppermost and indispensable. A decision is free and rational.

This distinction is illustrated in the biblical episode that features Phinehas in an act of zealotry. The people of Israel were engaged in harlotry and idolatry, enticed and captivated by the beautiful women of Moab. Phinehas was devastated by the scene of abomination enacted in public, and in a moment of zealotry, notwithstanding that he was risking his life because it was threatened by the enraged multitude, he put to death two flagrant violators of fundamental biblical precepts forbidding such conduct. This act of zealotry was entirely an emotional reaction to what the Torah regards as a detestable state of affairs. Of considerable significance is a talmudic discussion of a certain variation in response to a situation similar to the one encountered by Phinehas. The Talmud poses the question of a Jew asking the court, under identical circumstances, whether he is permitted to act as Phinehas did. Would he be allowed to do so? The answer given was negative.[11] If he is seeking to justify an act of zealotry on rational grounds, he is informed that due process must be applied. The Talmud accordingly distinguishes the emotional reaction from the rational response in a morally challenging situation.

Accordingly, if the action is merely the inevitable outcome of a struggle between an emotion attached to a value and an emotion generated organically, if it is merely the resultant of opposing emotional forces, then we cannot speak of a person acting in freedom and exercising rational control over his actions. But Judaism believes in human freedom and in the human capacity to exercise control, at least over his moral life. Judaism holds that the person, the spiritual element in the human being, the soul, possesses the power to resist the force of emotion, no matter what its strength, and to act in a manner that accords with the values to which he is committed.

The talmudic sages recognized the difficulties involved in conducting one's life in a free and rational manner and outlined a procedure to strengthen resolve when confronting temptation.

A man's good inclination should always engage the evil inclination in battle. If it is victorious, well and good; if not, let him engage in the study of Torah. . . . If he is then successful, well and good; if not, let him recite the *Keriat Shema*. . . . If he is successful, well and good; if not, let him bring to mind the day of his death.[12]

---

[11] *Mishneh Torah,* Hilchot Issurei Beah 12:5.
[12] Berachot 5a.

To strengthen an individual's resolution to activate the will rather than allow his emotions unrestrained control, it is necessary to deepen his appreciation of values through the recitation of *Keriat Shema* or the study of Torah, repositories of Jewish values. If this fails, the force of his emotions may be weakened further by contemplating his own death; but this is merely an aid. The individual, by virtue of the divine element within him, the spiritual dimension of his being, possesses the capacity to overrule his emotions no matter the force they exert.

Chapter 6

The Pursuit of Excellence

Perfection cannot be achieved by imperfect human beings. In *Ethics of the Fathers* we are told, "You are not required to complete the task, but you are not free to withdraw from it." This commentary is usually interpreted as dealing with the study of Torah. If it were possible to acquire perfect knowledge of Torah, we would not be relieved of the responsibility of doing so. The meaning is that it is impossible, in Torah study, to realize perfection. A similar judgment is available in Ecclesiastes with respect to conduct: "There is no man on earth who is so righteous who does that which is good and never sins."[1] Even Moses is described as falling prey to human frailties. But while perfection is not a realistic human goal, excellence is. We will achieve it by pursuing the task even if it is impossible to complete.

But what is excellence; how shall we define it? The quality of excellence needs to be characterized in both an ethical and a moral sense. It is related to the development of traits that contribute to well-being (the ethical goal) as well as the cultivation of attitudes and dispositions that translate into responsible and

---

[1] Ecclesiastes 3:20.

constructive human relations (the moral goal). Its definition ultimately depends on the ideal that supplies the criterion for its characterization. In ancient days, and according to one great thinker, excellence, or virtue, was described as the possession of qualities and dispositions and the performance of actions that lead to human happiness. Happiness has been defined alternatively as a balanced life in which all of a person's faculties function harmoniously, as a life of pleasure, or as a tranquil life unperturbed by any traumatic events that might otherwise lead to suffering and agony. It has been defined, in the Jewish religious context, as a life of piety and the observance of *mitzvot*. These are ethical goals which, according to their advocates, lead to personal well-being.

Judaism, however, gives priority to its moral sense. It identifies human excellence, as explained above, with *imitatio Dei*, the imitation of God, a cardinal precept derived from the biblical mandate *vehalachta bidruchov*, "you shall walk in His ways."[2] This concept, however, requires clarification. God is transcendent; that is, He is inscrutable and ineffable. No words in our language can adequately describe or characterize the Divine Being. He is categorically unique. The attempt to imitate God presents the Jew with insoluble problems. Maimonides undertook to resolve this dilemma by offering the following as the meaning of "You shall walk in His ways":

Just as He is called gracious, so shall you be gracious; just as He is called compassionate so shall you be compassionate; just as He is called holy, so shall you be holy. The prophets in this manner described the Almighty by all the various attributes: long-suffering, abundant in mercy,

---

[2] Deuteronomy 28:9. Another source of this principle is *lulechet bechol deruchuv*, ibid. 11:22.

righteous and upright, perfect, mighty and powerful, and
so on, to teach us that these qualities are good and right,
and a man is obligated to conduct himself accordingly
and to imitate Him with all his strength.[3]

Note the carefully formulated language. Maimonides is not
saying that just as God *is* gracious, so shall we be gracious, but
just as God is *called* gracious, so shall we *be* gracious. It is
impossible to delineate any of the attributes of an infinite and
inscrutable God in terms applicable to man. We must rely on
the prophetic descriptions of the Supreme Being, whose main
purpose is to communicate to us those qualities that are good
and right, which a man is obligated to appropriate into his
character with all his strength. It should be observed that the
religious objective, according to this account, is not merely to
cultivate certain moral qualities, but to imitate God as much as
it is humanly possible, for it is such conduct, accompanied by
the appropriate intent, that fosters a relationship with the
Divine Being, the goal of the religious personality. This is the
ultimate aim for which the Jew is obligated, by biblical precept,
to strive, and this is the goal of excellence that a Jew is mandated to pursue.

It is noteworthy that this biblical mandate is interpreted in
the Talmud in moral rather than ethical terms. The Torah
requires that we shall walk in His ways, but this commandment could be fulfilled in a variety of ways. He creates, and so
shall we; He is wise, and so shall we strive for wisdom. The
ability to create and the acquisition of wisdom can be interpreted in purely ethical terms; they can be understood as referring to personal qualities which an individual, for the sake of

---

[3] *Mishneh Torah*, Hilchot Deot 1:6. Compare this formulation with the
one in Shabbat 133b.

his well-being, seeks to possess.[4] Yet, in interpreting the biblical command that "you shall walk in His ways," the talmudic sages preferred to do so in moral terms. "Be like Him; as He is gracious and compassionate, so shall you be gracious and compassionate."[5] They did not place emphasis on personal attributes, such as wisdom, freedom, the capacity to create, and so on, but on gracious and compassionate conduct in interpersonal relationships.

In any case, the excellence for whose attainment man ought to strive is primarily to imitate God in His moral ways even while not neglecting imitation in connection with the development of personal virtues. In doing so, prompted by the desire to be like Him, man achieves his primary goal, namely, to have a relationship with Him.

I

An implication of the pursuit of excellence is that the Jew who embraces it is always in a state of dissatisfaction, even when he has accumulated an impressive record of accomplishments. There is a large gap, perhaps even a chasm, separating excellence from perfection, and there is always room for further progress. In addition, there is no specific well-defined point which can be identified as *the* level of excellence that one must reach to experience satisfaction; hence it is impossible for an individual to claim that he has achieved it. Further, the judgment of excellence depends on a context. There is no doubt that Archimedes achieved excellence in the pursuit of scientific

---

[4] In fact, these characterizations of the Divine Being and the obligation of imitation they impose on man are sometimes offered as interpretations of the biblical assertion to the effect that man was created in the image of God. See Rabbi Joseph B. Soloveitchik, *The Lonely Man of Faith*, sec. III, C.

[5] Shabbat 133b.

knowledge in ancient days, as did Kepler and Galileo in modern times. Given the scientific information available at the time, their accomplishments were phenomenal, but what they did merely provided the springboard for further scientific developments in our own day. To achieve excellence today, we must aim higher still. Excellence, therefore, is relative; the one who pursues it is perennially dissatisfied.

To be perpetually dissatisfied with our own moral and religious life is the essence of the consciousness of sin. It is not only the frequent violator of halachic precepts, assuming that he has some religious sensitivity, who experiences inadequacy in virtue of his many transgressions; it is also the very pious and scholarly student of Torah who does so, because he knows, even if he cannot identify them, that he is not free of sins. His sense of sin is usually more pronounced than that of the perennial transgressor because of his profound commitment to Torah, his more detailed awareness of the obligations it imposes, and his greater responsiveness. The requirement of penitence, which is mandatory throughout the year but especially during the High Holiday season, sensitizes the religious Jew and prompts him to contemplate and assess his actions, which inevitably leads to a sense of dissatisfaction.

Dissatisfaction is essential to personal growth, morally and religiously. In an informal conversation, Rabbi Joseph B. Soloveitchik responded to the question "What is the fundamental difference between the Jew of today, who is frequently lax in observance, and the Jew of the past, who was meticulous in fulfilling the commandments?" by saying, "The Jew of the past was dissatisfied, while the contemporary Jew is satisfied." Indeed, to be in a state of dissatisfaction provides the motivation to strive for an improved state of affairs that will yield greater, though not total, satisfaction.

On the biblical phrase *vayeshev yaakov*, "and Jacob dwelt," taking the word *vayeshev* to connote the quality of serenity, Rashi comments, "The righteous sought to live in a state of tranquility, so the Almighty said to them, Is not that which is prepared for you in the world to come sufficient?"[6] The intent here is that in the world here and now, the righteous must always live in a state of dissatisfaction, because human ideals have not been perfectly realized and acts of injustice are rampant. Therefore, either a person is not righteous and is consequently indifferent to the evils that surround him, or if he is, he cannot be apathetic to the afflictions suffered by others and thus must be dissatisfied.

II

But further, the gap that an individual in a state of dissatisfaction observes is not between his accomplishments and the state of *excellence*, but between his accomplishments and the goal of *perfection*. It is said that Isaac Newton, who formulated the theory of gravity, and whose standing as a scientist was, for centuries, beyond compare, described his achievement as like that of finding a sea shell on the seashore while the vast ocean of truth lay uncharted before him. It is such an awareness, derived from the contrast between what is and what ought to be, namely, the perfect or the ideal, that instills within the individual a depth of dissatisfaction that is the basis for a motivation powerful enough to drive the individual forward to excellence.

Religions are sometimes credited with providing their adherents with feelings of tranquility, with peace of mind. Such may be the case with other faiths, but it is entirely incompatible with Jewish doctrine. The Jew always lives in a state of tension. What is the nature of that tension? Rabbi Joseph B. Soloveitchik maintained that it is a consequence of the contradiction that is experienced when one is drawn in two opposite but equally

---

[6] Genesis 37:2.

legitimate directions. He conceived it as a perpetual internal struggle between man's drive toward self-assertion expressed in creativity and control, on the one hand, and the need to submit totally and selflessly to the will of God, on the other. It is not possible to be preoccupied with both simultaneously; and whenever one finds oneself at one of these poles, one feels drawn to the other.[7] But there is another source of tension which is the basis for ongoing and uninterrupted creativity, namely, the dissatisfaction experienced by an individual in virtue of the fact that whatever his achievements may be, even if they are spectacular, they can never reach the perfect or the ideal.

But more, it is important to note a distinction between the perfect and the ideal. The ideal includes perfection, but it contains something additional, for not everything perfect is also ideal. There is the notion of a perfect automobile, a perfect garment, a perfect baseball game, but none of these is viewed as ideal. The term "ideal" is normally used in reference to *values* when they are conceived in perfect form. But, as noted above, there are two sets of values: the *ethical*, which are deduced from ideals that project goals for individual well-being, such as knowledge and health; and the *moral*, which derive from ideals that prescribe conduct in interpersonal relations, such as honesty and justice.

Moral ideals are especially significant because they, but not ethical ideals, are essential components of the state of redemption for which mankind always strives. The pursuit of ethical ideals is irrelevant to redemption unless, as in the case of knowledge, its accumulation can be utilized to advance moral goals. The great cook, the celebrated sportsman, the brilliant chess player earn deserved reputations for excellence which may very well contribute to their sense of well-being, but they

----

[7] *Lonely Man of Faith*, sec. IX, C.

do not contribute to a utopian forward march. The pursuit of moral ideals does. The messianic era is always interpreted in terms of the perfect exemplification in society and for all mankind of the moral ideals of mercy, justice, and peace. It is the comparison between what has been achieved and the perfect, but even more the contrast with the ideal that provides the inspiration to pursue the kind of excellence that has redemptive potential.

There are two words in the Hebrew language that underscore the distinction between ethical and moral ideals. One is *shleimut* and the other *temimut*. The first refers to perfection in the form of personal attainments, the ethical goal. The patriarch Jacob, having been separated from his parents for two decades, having sent gifts in abundance to his brother Esau to pacify him, and having engaged an angel in a physical contest that left him crippled, is reported as returning to Shechem in a condition described as *shuleim*,[8] "whole" or "complete." Rashi comments that he was whole in his knowledge of Torah, notwithstanding the two decades that he spent with his idolatrous father-in-law Laban; whole in body, despite the injuries he sustained in his struggle with the angel; and complete in wealth, having apparently replaced the substantial material goods he presented to Esau. These forms of perfection have to do with personal development, achievement in the pursuit of ethical goals. *Temimut* refers to perfection in relationships with others through the application in these interactions of the principles of truth, justice, mercy, and piety.[9] Commitment to an ideal is the finest source of inspiration in the struggle to achieve excellence.

---

[8] Genesis 33:18.

[9] Rabbi Naftali Tzvi Yehuda Berlin, in his commentary on the Torah, explains the phrase *veyaakov ish tam* (Genesis, 25:27) "and Jacob was complete," to mean *mutamem im anashim*, he was perfect in his relations with others. The connection between *tam* and *temimut* is obvious.

III

Ideals translate into the values which, should they inspire commitment, will be exemplified in conduct. The ideal of justice is embodied in such values as fulfilling debt obligations, respect for privacy, compensation for injury caused, and returning objects that are found. The ideal of truth entails such values as objectivity in judgment, detachment from personal interests, and the primacy of reason. The pursuit of excellence can also be understood as an active commitment to values that flow from ideals.

It should be noted that values can be, and are by some, interpreted *subjectively*, that is, they are perceived as expressive of personal feelings. The value assigned to them is seen as coincident with individual desire, with the consequence that one person's values may differ from another's. One could maintain, to the contrary, that if something is judged to be deserving of the honorific term *value*, it must be *objective*, that is, it must be understood as emerging from the word of the Divine Being, or, and this has been suggested by many even from a religious perspective, it must be inherent in the very nature of things. Nature could then be understood in terms of imperatives or intuitions inscribed in the human mind,[10] but it could also be interpreted in terms of demands imposed by society on individuals to ensure its viability. On this interpretation, the ideal justice and the values into which this ideal translates would be accepted as a divine prescription or as derived from some objective ground. According to this theory of objective values, a distinction can appropriately be made between needs and values. Needs are subjective, they are manifestations of an individual's physical or psychological impulses; values are objec-

---

[10] See Rabbi Meir Simcha Hakohen of Dvinsk, *Meshech Chachmah*, Deuteronomy 30:11–14.

tive. A dispute could even arise with regard to the same act as to whether it is to be interpreted as a response to a need or the embodiment of a value. One could, for example, explain the desirability of the institution of marriage in terms of the satisfaction of normal physiological urges and the dissipation of loneliness (the subjective interpretation) or as the fulfillment of values such as procreation and the development of a family that will carry forward cherished traditions (the objective interpretation). Such a distinction was once suggested at a conference on marriage, and a secularist responded by noting that the satisfaction of needs is also a value. He was expressing a different conception of values, which holds that values need not be objective. On his view, a value is anything that is cherished or wanted. If one has adopted a philosophy of moral egoism or individual hedonism, for example, then immediate satisfaction of spontaneous impulses may be regarded as a value, and indeed, the ultimate value. On the interpretation of values advocated here, importance attached to objects arising out of an individual's subjective feelings and dispositions is not a value.

The subjective enterprise, the determination to satisfy needs, may also give rise to dissatisfaction. An individual deprived of opportunities for pleasure may experience frustration and strive with energy and passion to find occasions that will provide nourishment for his sensuous appetites. Since one who pursues pleasure never has enough of it, the dissatisfaction may be persistent. He too will be inspired to seek it in its perfect form, which cannot be realized anymore than an ideal. In this instance too, as in the case of the pursuit of values, he will fall short of its possession. But he may also fall short in his effort because, very often, perfection does not provide an incentive as powerful as does the ideal and the values that flow from it.

The difference between a subjective and an objective goal is the appropriateness of calculation. How much effort, how much pain, normally associated with resolve and determination is one prepared to endure to enjoy, for example, a specific quantity of pleasure. If, upon calculation, a person determines that the quantity of pain exceeds the anticipated pleasure, he will refrain from the effort. Effort inspired by an ideal, on the other hand, can be almost infinite in magnitude. No matter what the difficulty and even the agony, if the commitment is strong and inflexible, the pursuit continues. The people of Israel have been dreaming and striving for the arrival of the messianic era in which mankind will live in justice and uninterrupted peace, and despite tragic circumstances endured over millennia, they continue to do so. They remain enchanted by the ideal and drawn to it without resignation; calculation is irrelevant.

The relentless pursuit of excellence has been a distinctive character of the Jewish people because Judaism has not been preoccupied with motivating its adherents to action on the basis of considerations of self-interest. The experience of pleasure for example, while unobjectionable, has not been a Jewish thrust across the centuries. The reason is that the Bible and Talmud require the organization of a society that is obligation-oriented. A rights-oriented society may be concerned primarily with the satisfaction of needs. Judaism justifies human effort to fulfill basic human needs on the grounds that a satisfactory response to the demands of impulse is prerequisite to the business of living, but the Jew is required to go beyond this. An obligation-oriented society is based on a set of precepts prescribing duties that reflect perennial obligations to God and man. This is a consequence of the primacy of *mitzvot*, commandments, in Jewish life. The Jewish pursuit of excellence, therefore, has been a manifestation of a commitment to the realization of values above and beyond the satisfaction of needs, and the tireless determination to come ever closer, not merely to perfection, but to the attainment of ideals.

IV

There is another condition indispensable to the pursuit of moral excellence, namely, a belief that ultimately the goal can be achieved, though probably not in one's lifetime. This reflects Judaism's spirit of optimism about human life on earth. It would be difficult to strive for so this-worldly an ideal if there were no conviction that it is realizable.

Of course, there are different kinds of optimism. One of its forms is based on an inference from observed facts, and another is based on faith. If an army, engaged in a military campaign, brings to the battlefield troops that are better trained, better equipped, and more numerous, hope of victory is certainly justified in the light of the situation that prevails. If the facts fail to validate the hope, there is despair, as illustrated in the biblical episode of the spies. When they rendered a report that the land of Canaan was impregnable and beyond the possibility of conquest, the people reacted with total resignation. The hopelessness conveyed by the report resulted in paralysis. But to preserve optimism in the face of facts that suggest a high probability of failure requires faith. This is the kind of optimism that has been characteristic of the people of Israel in their often frustrating and occasionally tragic odyssey across the centuries. An outstanding example is, of course, the resurrection of the Jewish state after a painful hiatus of two millennia. It is evident that optimism with respect to the attainability of the goal— whether supported by facts or by faith—is conducive to the preservation of resolve to achieve it.

Just as important as the belief that the goal is attainable is the feeling of a people— as individuals and as a collectivity—that they have the capacity to contribute to its realization. This is implied by the biblical declaration that man was created in the image of God. Man is not weak and powerless; he is a creature abundantly endowed with skills, talents, intellectual prowess, creative ability, and a sense of self-sufficiency and self-determination capable of building the world he envisions. He has the competence, and if he also has the inclination, progress is assured, though all too often, with some, the redemptive will is lacking, leading to patterns of history that are not encouraging. This, however, should not, and indeed does not, dissuade the Jewish people from maintaining resolve and investing energy to press forward on the path to redemption. We may not reach it, but we will get closer.

V

We return to the distinction between moral and ethical values. As was noted above, ethical values are concerned with the development of excellences in the human personality, while those designated moral are excellences in interpersonal relationships. It needs to be added that moral values are substantially different from those that are ethical. In fact, the two are largely independent of each other.

From a purely logical standpoint, the acquisition of moral virtues is not at all functionally dependent on the possession of those that are ethical. It does not follow that a person seeking excellence in his personal life would necessarily strive to cultivate moral virtues. Such a connection has been argued in the course of the history of ideas. It has been maintained that a person who is interested in his own welfare would inevitably conduct himself morally in relation to others, that is, he would cultivate moral virtues in order to improve the quality of his own life. He would be happier in a society guided by moral precepts than in one that is morally chaotic, and his own moral conduct would serve as a paradigm to inspire others to moral behavior. The logic is flawed; it is not logically compelling that if any given individual conducts himself morally the moral character of society will be enhanced. Nor does it follow that if a person engages in undetected criminal behavior the moral quality of society will deteriorate. Nor is there a causal, empirical, connection between ethical and moral conduct. It is not indicated, via experience, that those who pursue excellences of the ethical variety also engage in an effort to develop moral virtues. It is certain that many conduct themselves in a manner that makes it obvious that they do not see any connection, logical or otherwise, between moral conduct and personal happiness.

It is clear, therefore, that the pursuit of ethical excellence does not necessitate moral conduct or social progress. Nor, in the reverse, can it be logically inferred that someone who conducts himself morally will simultaneously exert himself to cultivate attitudes that will yield personal well-being, though he obviously deserves it. There are many in the Jewish community who neglect their own interests and the cultivation of attitudes that can lead to what is popularly identified as happiness and who devote themselves to the achievement of moral and religious goals. The Talmud hints at this state of affairs by raising the question of *yesh tzaddik vera lo yesh rasha vetov lo,* "there are righteous who suffer and scoundrels who prosper."[11] The talmudic solution to the problem is that, while commitment to moral and religious excellence does not involve, logically or causally, a life of unparalleled well-being, there is a Providence which will ultimately reward the pious and punish the guilty, if not in this world then in the world to come. Those who devote themselves to the service of God and man, and neglect their own well-being which eventuates in a life of pain, are assured happiness in the afterlife.

Notwithstanding, it can be argued, and I believe cogently, that if the objectivity of moral values is understood as based on divine imperatives, the focused attempt to develop moral virtues will lead to the acquisition of ethical excellencies as well— not because of some intimate connection, logical or empirical, between the two, but because both are rooted in the

---

[11] Berachot 7a.

same divine source. One who accepts moral values divinely prescribed will accept all commandments, including those intended to enhance the development of personality and the achievement of well-being, such as "You shall rejoice before the Lord, your God."

Chapter 7

Human Dignity

The recognition that human beings are endowed with dignity and the consequential obligation to treat others with respect is a paramount imperative. It emerges in a variety of talmudic discourses, among which the following is basic: "Great is the rule requiring respect for human beings, for it overrides a precept of Torah." An inquiry follows

> How is this possible? "There is a rule: There is neither wisdom nor understanding nor counsel against the Lord" [i.e., one may not for human reasons suspend a biblical obligation]. Rav ben Shaba proceeded to explain the principle: "It refers to the [biblical] precept 'Thou shalt not deviate.' " His colleagues objected to this explanation on the grounds that this precept too is a biblical command. Rabbi Kahana replied, "All the ordinances of the rabbis were based by them on the prohibition 'Thou shalt not deviate,' but where the question of human dignity is concerned, the rabbis allowed the act [which they otherwise prohibited].[1]

---

[1] Berachot 19b.

According to Rabbi Kahana's clarification, the principle that allows the suspension of *mitzvot* in the interests of human dignity refers to those of rabbinic origin. Now while it is true that rabbinic precepts have as their principal source of sanction a Torah command, namely, "Thou shalt not deviate," rabbinic principles of conduct are still to be distinguished from those that are explicitly biblical, and it is the former, according to Rabbi Kahana, that may be suspended to safeguard human dignity.

Why, then, in the formulation of the principle, is it declared that human dignity overrides a Torah precept rather than merely rabbinic precepts? The talmudic sages clearly sought to underscore and dramatize the importance of human dignity. They did so, in the first place, by referring to the biblical underpinning of rabbinic precepts rather than their merely rabbinic character. In addition, they did so because of their understanding that the requirements of human dignity do at times suspend even explicit biblical commands. This is the case when the precept is positive rather than negative and its implementation can be avoided passively, by inaction. Rashi elaborates:

> There are many things that justify uprooting a Torah principle, such as the need to make a fence around the law or to preserve human dignity. But this applies only when one does not violate a principle through action but remains in his place and the Torah precept is violated by itself.[2]

The assertion that "The rule requiring respect for the human being is great because it overrides a precept of Torah," therefore, includes the passive suspension of a positive Torah precept. The emphasis on overriding a Torah precept rather than those merely rabbinic is accordingly appropriate.

---

[2] Ibid. 20a.

But there is still another consideration that justifies the articulation of this principle in terms of the suspension of a Torah precept, namely, that the Torah itself, according to rabbinic interpretation, introduced exceptions to some of its laws and indeed formulated some of them in such a way as to give recognition and emphasis to the importance of human dignity. There is, for example, the biblical imperative to return to its owner an object that is lost and to avoid the inclination to turn away from it. The Talmud notes the following exception: If the finder is a sage, and it is not consistent with his status to lead a straying horse through the streets, for example, he is relieved of the obligation—that is, he may turn away. The Talmud directs attention to a certain peculiarity in the formulation of the biblical precept to restore a lost object to its owner. In the same passage, it is stated, "You shall not see your brother's ox or his sheep gone astray, and you shall avoid it." It is an ambiguous verse subject to contrary interpretations. The discussion proceeds as follows:

There are times when you may hide yourself from them and times when you may not hide yourself from them. How so? . . . If he is an elder and it is not in accordance with his dignity. . . . Therefore it is said, "and you shall avoid" [a phrase in the biblical passage which seems to suggest that one should turn away]. But why so? Let us apply the rule "There is no wisdom nor understanding nor counsel against the Lord." The case is different there, because it says expressly, "and you shall hide yourself from them." Let us then derive from this. [There is a rule that if a person discovers that he is wearing a garment that is prohibited because it is made from a combination of wool and linen, he must remove it even if he is in a public place and will suffer embarrassment. The question is: Should not the principle of human dignity in this instance too warrant the suspension of a Torah precept?]

We do not derive a ritual rule from a rule relating to property [wearing a prohibited garment does not involve a
financial obligation vis-à-vis another, whereas refraining
from returning a lost object does].[3]

In this discussion it is noted that a verse intended primarily
to prohibit an individual from avoiding his obligation to return
a lost object is formulated in such a way as to allow the deduction that in instances of this type, namely, where the demand of
human dignity is urgent and the issue is financial rather than
ritual, the Torah itself suspended the obligation. The Torah
accordingly introduced an exception because of considerations
of human dignity. Here then is another application of the principle that the preservation of human dignity overrides a Torah
obligation.

The general principle "The rule requiring respect for human
beings is great because it overrides a Torah precept" accordingly directs attention to a variety of halachic imperatives—
mostly rabbinic but some explicitly biblical—and, by its very
formulation, accentuates the overarching importance of preserving human dignity as a rule guiding conduct in the life of
both the individual and society.

I

The first requirement imposed by the principle of human
dignity is that each human being shall perceive himself as distinctive and unique and of surpassing value. Man is categorically different from all the other beings that inhabit the planet.
This is declared in a beautiful prayer that is recited as part of
the *Neilah* service of *Yom Kippur*. It begins with the phrase "You
have separated man from the first and considered him worthy
to stand in Your presence." The notion of *havdalah*, which

---

[3] Ibid. 19b.

declares that man is separate and apart, does not merely refer to distinctive physical traits. He is not separated from the rest of creation as one species of animal is from another in virtue of possessing differentiating biological features. There are no valuational inequalities among animals to reflect their biological differences. It is the sense of the phrase "You have separated man from the first," that man is distinguished from the remainder of existence not merely by way of a different and perhaps more complex organic structure but primarily because he possesses value.

There are different bases for separation and the assignment of value. One may derive the elevated status of man, which translates into the sense of human dignity, from a variety of considerations. Throughout the history of human thought, men have felt deeply that there is something extraordinary about the human being that sets him far apart and above other species. Some have associated it with his capacity to reason;[4] some have identified it with his power of speech;[5] others argue that it is rooted in his freedom;[6] still others that it is derived from creativity.[7] Each of these views is expressed in terms that are appealing even to the secular mind, but for the religious individual man's special quality is expressed in the idea that man is created in the image of God. The latter notion is interpreted in terms of characteristics, some of which are here enumerated, which single him out and place him in an elevated category.

---

[4] Rashi on Genesis 1:26.

[5] In a modern version of the view, Susan K. Langer, in her *Philosophy in a New Key*, characterized man as *homo symbolicum*; that is, he is a being that uses language. The close relation between the power of reason and the power of speech does not require elaboration.

[6] Rabbi Samson R. Hirsch expressed this view in his commentary on Genesis 1:26.

[7] Rabbi Joseph B. Soloveitchik, in *The Lonely Man of Faith*, associates this view with the biblical command *vechibshuha* (Genesis 1:28), which means, take control of the world through creativity.

Even a philosophical hedonist who believes that the only thing worth pursuing is pleasure, that is, that pleasure is the ultimate good, can affirm this doctrine of separation and valuation. When asked: "If pleasure is the only good, in what way does man differ from the animal, since both are prodded to pursue pleasure?" one utilitarian and hedonistic thinker responded, as already noted in these pages, by saying that the human being prefers pleasures that are commensurate with human dignity. Man will often forgo physical satisfactions, such as eating, drinking, and indulging in carnal delights, in favor of the pleasures of contemplation, literature, music, and art.[8] Now, notwithstanding that this view presented him with a logical inconsistency—for if it is indeed correct, then human dignity rather than pleasure is the ultimate good—he could not resist embracing the doctrine that man was "separated from the first."

According to the author of the *Neilah* prayer, the fundamental basis for the division is none of the above. It is, rather, the special relationship that man has to the Supreme Being, a relation not limited to the Jew. Everyone in the human family has the capacity to enter into it, and that potential is, in the perspective of the religious individual, the source of human dignity. In the halachic conception, the Jew is also separated from the rest of mankind, and that separation arises out of a dimension of sanctity that is rooted in the Covenant. The fact that the Jew at Sinai made a covenantal commitment to God and assumed the obligation to live by six hundred and thirteen commandments, brought him a degree of sanctity that others may acquire only by a similar covenantal undertaking, which in effect is a gesture of conversion. There exists, accordingly, a basis for separation that is based on sanctity.

---

[8] John Stuart Mill, in *Utilitarianism* (New York: Liberal Arts Press, 1953), p. 10.

Our concern at present, however, is not the differentiation of the Jew from mankind as a result of sanctity, but that of man from the rest of creation that is based on dignity. It is noteworthy that the prayer of *Yom Kippur* does not say, "You have separated the Jew from the time of Abraham with whom You entered into a special Covenant" or "You have separated the Jew from the day when he entered into the Sinaitic Covenant," but "You have separated man from the first." All men are endowed with human dignity.

There are philosophical doctrines that deny the principle of separation and concomitantly deprive the individual of the character of human dignity. One outstanding example is the theory of evolution, which has always presented an onerous challenge to religious thinkers. The essential problem this theory presents to the religious mind, however, is not so much the fact that its description of the emergence of man disagrees with the process of creation as depicted in the book of Genesis. It is, rather, that by insisting that man emerged out of lower forms of animal existence, it places man and animal in the same category, that is, it fails to affirm the principle of separation and its concomitant, the exalted status of the human being. Another philosophical doctrine that finds itself in the identical situation is materialism, a view which affirms that everything, including man, consists exclusively of matter devoid of a soul. Communism, with its dogma of dialectical materialism, maintained such a view. The implications are that man differs from the animal or a clod of earth in no fundamental way.

Such views can lead to denying human beings that sense of dignity which, on the religious view, is essential to the very definition of humanity. They can also lead, and indeed have, to the dehumanization of large segments of mankind with inevitable attendant atrocities.

II

It has already been noted that the doctrine of the dignity of man affirms not merely that man is separated from the rest of creation but that he possesses inherent value not shared by other segments of creation. This value, which derives from the fact that man is created in God's image, confers upon mankind the status of a moral community. A moral community is one which demands that mutual respect, arising precisely out of the conviction that man has intrinsic value, shall be displayed among all its members. The nature of this respect, however, needs to be characterized because there is more than one variety.

Power also inspires respect. Power, of course, can manifest itself in destructive as well as creative ways. In its destructive form, it intimidates and destroys, and the reaction it elicits could more appropriately be described as fear, though it may be argued that fear too is a form of respect, or at least inspires it. In its constructive manifestation, it invents and creates and does elicit widespread and profound respect. Such is the power of the physician, the engineer, the architect, the jurist, the business executive, and the philanthropist. Each utilizes the power of the intellect, talent, personality, and even substance to improve the lives of individuals and society, and in the process earns endless respect and appreciation.

The differences between these two varieties of respect are several. In the first place, respect for creative power is a response to that which is instrumental in nature; respect for value is a recognition of something that deserves to be cherished that is intrinsic in character. The appreciation prompted by scientific and technological achievements is a function of the advantages perceived to flow from them. We admire those who are sources of blessing for mankind and who improve the quality of human life. One philosopher maintained that knowledge is power, that is, its principal purpose is to enable mankind to solve the many problems that inevitably confront it. Another argued that even the invention of a form of mathematics which at the time of its appearance has no apparent earthly use is essentially of instrumental value because it is anticipated that eventually it will indeed be applied, as in fact it has, in the practical arena.

The other variety of respect is inspired by that which is perceived to possess intrinsic value. It depends on no advantages to be accrued, on no benefits to be received; a human being is respected because he is endowed with a quality in virtue of which he is a member of the moral community. Another way of making this point is to assert, using Kantian terminology, that a human being is not to be regarded as a means to something else that is of value, but always as an end in himself. Human beings are not to be used; other things are to be used as instruments for man's benefit.

We may illustrate the distinction between perceiving man as instrumental and as possessing inherent value by directing attention to the debate concerning triage. When medical resources are inadequate to provide treatment to all who require it, a problem arises as to who is to be assigned priority. One may, in formulating a response, display respect for power by deciding to allocate medicine and treatment to those who possess greater power, that is, the potential to contribute maximally to family and society. This is the instrumental approach. Or, as Judaism prescribes, one may exhibit respect for intrinsic human value, in which case, the practical potential of the patient is irrelevant and all must be regarded as equally deserving. On the latter view, everyone who comes to the physician's attention must receive treatment and in the sequence in which they appear.

The concept of inherent value is applicable in other contexts as well. There is a biblical obligation to respect parents. Some relate this duty to the degree of success that parents achieve in the course of their lives or at least to the contributions parents make to the well-being of their progeny. In the absence of such accomplishments, it is argued, respect is misplaced. This is repugnant to the Jewish view. A parent is to be respected essentially because of his status as a parent irrespective of the practical, instrumental aspects of his life.

The doctrine of the dignity of man requires the same kind of response to man in general. The respect due to the human being is a result of his intrinsic value, because he possesses a character that makes him deserving of it, a character which in religious terms is interpreted as a manifestation of the divine image. It is independent of achievement or the lack thereof or even of antisocial behavior. A criminal is also deserving of it.

> Yochanan ben Zakkai declared: Come and see how great is the rule obligating respect for man. An ox that walks on his own legs [if it is sold or slaughtered by the thief who stole it], five [i.e., the thief must pay five times the value of the ox]; a lamb that needs to be carried, four.[9]

One way of demonstrating respect is by taking into account the amount of pain suffered by a thief in the very process of committing a crime. It is apparently less difficult to steal an ox, because it can be dragged with a rope, than a lamb, which needs to be carried. The point is that even a criminal is a member of the moral community and deserves consideration, because he too is a bearer of the divine image. Human value must be taken into account even when considering the act of theft. In any case, this discussion provides an outstanding example of the principle that respect is owed a human being irrespective of what he does, but essentially because of what he is.

---

[9] Baba Kamma 79b.

Since human life possesses intrinsic value, respect for a human being constitutes a moral obligation whether he is within or outside the Jewish community. By halachic criteria, the non-Jew has a powerful claim on the respect of the Jew. Consider the following passage from Maimonides' code:

> All these principles [which guide the conduct of the Jewish judge] will depend on the judge's perception that they are appropriate to the individual and the circumstances. All his actions shall be for the sake of heaven; nor shall the dignity of man be slight in his eyes, because it allows for the suspension of a negative rabbinic precept. And this is certainly the case with respect to the dignity of the children of Abraham, Isaac, and Jacob who adhere to the true Torah.[10]

Maimonides appears to allow more respect for the Jew than the non-Jew, not because the Jew's moral status as a human being demands it, but because the Jew is committed to the Torah—he is a member of the covenantal community and consequently possesses an added dimension of sanctity. Nevertheless, it is clear, on Maimonides' view, that all humans are deserving of respect.

Human dignity is possessed, in the halachic perspective, even by the human being who is no longer among the living. There is a talmudic concept entitled *kvod hamet*, the respect that is due to the dead. Many rules and guidelines prescribe the conduct necessary in relation to those who have departed. By and large, the vast majority of these rules and guidelines can be traced to the obligation to show respect for the dead, that is, to exhibit *kvod hamet*. But this principle is, at bottom, a subcategory of the generic principle of *kevod habriot*, giving respect to the

---

[10] *Mishneh Torah*, Hilchot Sanhedrin 24:10.

human being in virtue of the dignity with which he is endowed. The following talmudic passage is illustrative of this point.

> Rava asked: The reading of the *Megillah* [mandatory on Purim] and the burial of one who was found dead along the way [a *met mitzvah*], which takes priority? Is it the reading of the *Megillah*, because it publicizes the miracle, or the burial of the dead found along the way, because of the dignity of man? After asking, he answered: The burial of the dead found along the way, because it was taught: "The rule obligating respect for man is great because it suspends a biblically prescribed negative commandment."[11]

It is to be noted that while it is a *mitzvah*, the fulfillment of a religious obligation, to participate in the burials of all who have passed away, it is especially obligatory, and therefore a greater *mitzvah*, to do so in the case of one who was found lifeless and has no known relatives to undertake the task. While the latter is given special halachic attention and is explicitly identified as a *met mitzvah*, the reason for the obligation to involve oneself in the interment of all departed is one and the same, namely, *kevod habriot*, the respect due to man.

III

There is another distinction to be drawn between respecting power and respecting value. Respect for the former is normally self-interested. I need not, at any moment, benefit directly from the contribution that a creative use of power makes to mankind, but if I can perceive such benefit as accruing to me or

---

[11] Megillah 3b.

any of my loved ones at any future date, the respect I display for the creator of the object that enhances human life is primarily prompted by the thought that I may profit from it. What is good for mankind is generally good for me. Respect for value, on the other hand, is independent of any considerations of self-interest. It is inspired by the perception that there is something worthy of being prized in the object that possesses it, that it is to be admired and appreciated on its own account.

This distinction is crucial to the understanding of many debates and controversies that are always current on mankind's agenda. It arises, for example, in the context of marriage. When troubles between husband and wife erupt, a resolution of their difficulties might be based on the perceivable benefits to the parties involved. If either of them, as a result of calculating the positives and negatives, concludes that on balance, and from a practical viewpoint, the continued relationship is not advantageous, he or she may decide to terminate it. This is precisely the kind of calculus that is responsible for the high percentage of divorces in American society. On the other hand, the assessment of the marital situation may be based, for example, on respect for the intrinsic value of the children whose well-being is dependent on the perpetuation of the marriage, or even on that of the mate with whom one is involved in the marital relation, in which case husband and wife will take whatever measures are necessary and feasible for the marriage to succeed. And even while halachic Judaism allows divorce, the appreciation of the intrinsic value of human beings and the obligation to display disinterested commitment to the welfare of one's mate tend to keep marriages strong. It is because Jews in the past adopted this attitude that the marriage bond was relatively permanent and divorce very rare.

Recognition of the intrinsic value of human beings and the inclination to treat others in a disinterested way is equally important, though much more difficult, in the business community. The goal of business is profit, and one may easily deduce from this premise, with irrefutable logical rigor, that the sole basis for the relationship between employer and employee is the achievement of the business objective. The owner is interested in maximizing his profit, and if the employee fails in this regard, then woe unto him. The attitude inspired by the belief in human dignity is otherwise. There is an obligation the employer has to everyone he employs that is irrelevant to the profit motive. Two outstanding illustrations have, over the years, come to mind. The executives of a substantial corporation owned by a Jew sought a merger with one of America's largest and most prestigious business enterprises. Had that merger been effected, it would have been very disadvantageous to the employees of the smaller firm; their positions would have been at risk. The corporation's founder and creator intervened to prevent the merger on the grounds that, were it to materialize, many of his employees would lose their positions, resulting in irreparable harm to them and their families. A more recent instance involved the destruction by fire of a very large business enterprise. Its owner decided to maintain all his employees on salary during the period when the company's physical facilities were undergoing reconstruction, so that they would not suffer. These are dramatic manifestations of an unselfish regard for the dignity of man.

The recognition of the dignity of man and the concomitant obligation to relate to others in a disinterested manner is also required in the social arena. On the one hand, it is possible to adopt a collective stance and maintain that the interests of the individual are at all times to be subordinated to those of the community. Or, on the other, it is possible to adopt the reverse position and insist that the defense and protection of the individual is paramount, and that society, notwithstanding the injurious consequences it must endure as a result, may not interfere. On the former view, societal self-interest is the determining factor, and the individual must suffer if his needs are incompatible with the larger needs of the community. According to this approach, human dignity suffers. On the latter view, the respect due the individual in virtue of his intrinsic value overrides the community's claim.

It is one of the paradoxes of Jewish life that, even while it places great emphasis on the individual's obligation to the community, it assigns priority, in many instances, to the needs and well-being of the individual. The *halachah* strikes a balance between their respective claims and does not always demand the individual's subordination to community. The *halachah* recognizes the importance of the community and requires of the individual Jew that he acknowledge it as well. Halachic Judaism, for example, spells out a Jew's obligation to foster the performance of *mitzvot* by others (a communal obligation) and does so by promulgating the principle "All Jews are guarantors, one for another."[12] Nachmanides deduces a Jew's obligation to be concerned about the material possessions and honor of another from the fundamental principle, "Love your friend as yourself."[13] In addition, the Jewish people perceives itself as *bnai yisrael*, an integrated family all of whose members are descendants— physically or at least spiritually—of the patriarchs, a sentiment that heightens the sense of communal solidarity. The latter is also, according to the rabbis, a source of the imperative that requires a Jew to share in the pain of the community. All these precepts direct the Jew's attention to his community and obligate him to engage in action advantageous to it. Nevertheless, this communal consciousness is counterbalanced by a talmudic emphasis on the importance of the individual. The community may assess each of its members to contribute a specific amount to communal philanthropies, but it may not do so beyond a certain reasonable amount. It must

---

[12] Sanhedrin 27a.
[13] Commentary on Leviticus 19:18.

take into account the needs of the individual and his right to a dignified life.[14] The talmudic sages emphasized again and again that the life of one individual is equal in value to the lives of everyone in an entire community. If an enemy demanded that the community choose and surrender one of its members to be killed or the entire city would be annihilated, any attempt to designate such an individual would be halachically unacceptable.[15] This clearly demonstrates the respect and value that Judaism assigns to man. A community in this predicament may not selfishly sacrifice the life of even one individual to secure its own survival.

IV

The principle of *kvod habriot*, human dignity, accordingly implies that human beings occupy a special and elevated position, that this status is due to their possession of a characteristic that constitutes a reflection of the image of God, and consequently that they belong to a moral community in which they are entitled to the respect of their fellows, not because of instrumental and self-interested considerations but because of the intrinsic value of man.

Therefore, care must be taken, in all circumstances, to avoid embarrassing others. The teaching of the Mishnah is well known: "He who shames another in public has no share in the world to come." So serious an assault on human dignity is the infliction of humiliation on another, according to the Mishnah's precept, that the perpetrator is denied the *summum bonum*, the highest good promised in religious teaching. But, on the other hand and paradoxically, shame is sanctioned in circumstances in which an individual violates a moral or religious precept.

---

[14] Rema on Yoreh Deah 249:1.
[15] Jerusalem Talmud, Terumot, end of chap. 8.

Shame is not invariably incompatible with human dignity. To the contrary, the sense of human dignity may even require it. Indeed, it is precisely this sense that, in some contexts, renders the experience of embarrassment appropriate and even inevitable. Those who possess a sense of their own dignity recognize that there are moral and religious standards with which their conduct must be in accord. Especially is this the case if that sense of dignity is rooted in the belief that they bear the image of God, which requires that they conduct their lives in a manner that accords with divinely prescribed precepts. When they fail and fall short, they are inevitably embarrassed, an emotion which results from the perception that a chasm exists between their self-image and their conduct. Should others become aware of their transgression, their embarrassment is multiplied. Indeed, the feeling of humiliation is aggravated in a social context. If a rich man were to become impoverished and be deprived of his customary retinue of servants, he would feel embarrassment. If someone is discovered in violation of the law of the land, the normal emotional response is humiliation and even, if the transgression is sufficiently severe, disgrace. This is the case especially in circumstances where he strives to project an image of himself as a person of great integrity and as conscientiously law-abiding.

Placing another, by word or deed, in a situation of embarrassment is incompatible with the obligation to treat others with respect, but when a person is himself aware that he is in violation of a moral precept that expresses what he perceives as his exalted status, his sense that he is a dignified being translates into shame.

When Maimonides enumerates the essential components of repentance, he includes regret for what one did in the past, a confession of one's sin, and a resolution to avoid it in the future.[16] Maimonides does not count shame as one of the ingre-

---

[16] *Mishneh Torah*, Hilchot Teshuvah 2:2.

dients.[17] The reason is that shame is experienced spontaneously by a person who has a sense of human dignity; it does not
require special rabbinic legislation. A person who is aware of
himself as a member of the moral community inevitably experiences shame on the occasion of transgression. If the sense of
shame were absent, it would be impossible for him to perform
a genuine gesture of repentance. And it is precisely the sense of
human dignity that makes such an experience possible.

The very capacity to experience shame in circumstances of
moral and religious transgression is accounted a considerable
virtue. The rabbis teach that Jews have three characteristics.
They are prone to compassion, to shame, and to acts of kindness.

The experience of shame is the mark of a conscience that has
been violated because of a failure to comply with its standards,
a standard rooted in the sense of human dignity.

---

[17] He does, however, include it in the formula of the confession. A
penitent is required to declare, among other things, "I am embarrassed and humiliated because of my act" (ibid. 1:1).

Chapter 8

Joy

The quintessential problem of the study of ethics, at least in ancient days, was that of defining the *summum bonum*, the ultimate good, a goal toward which everyone seeking a good life would naturally strive. That goal was *happiness*. The philosophic schools supplied a variety of definitions of happiness that reveal the fundamental premises upon which their ethical theories were built. It is noteworthy that the element of pleasure played a central role in most of their characterizations. This was certainly the case for the Epicureans, who, like the modern hedonists and some utilitarians, explicitly identified happiness with pleasure. The Stoics, who defined happiness in terms of the ideal of imperturbability, also interpreted ethical goal in terms of pleasure. Since in their view, as a matter of fact, a balance of pleasure in one's lifetime was unattainable, the most one could hope for was to cope with the experience of pain by remaining unperturbed when confronting it, that is, by reducing the pain. Even the ancient master Aristotle, who identified happiness with the cultivation of the intellectual virtues, argued that pleasure is invariably superimposed on wisdom, which he identified as the ultimate human good.

Pleasure, however, does not enter into the definition of human happiness in the Jewish perspective. What is critical in the characterization of happiness for the Jew is *simchah*, joy. An analysis of the difference between joy and pleasure is essential for a clarification of the Jewish conception of happiness.

I

Pleasure and joy differ in their emotional anatomy. Pleasure is the satisfaction felt when one is engaged in gratifying experiences in a state of emotional insulation from others. It arises obviously in conditions of physical isolation when sensations are stimulated, generally in the course of acts of a biological nature, and often enough as concomitants of intellectual activity, such as reading a good book, or in aesthetic appreciation, such as listening to appealing music. But it is also experienced in contexts of human interaction. The isolation which is the matrix for the experience of pleasure is not of the physical but of the emotional variety. One may also experience pleasure in the process of engaging in activity with others—for example, in any of a variety of games, but the occurrence of such pleasures requires another human being merely as a feature of the circumstances in which pleasure is experienced; the other is not an essential component of the experience. In such instances, pleasure consists in the subjective, self-interested satisfaction associated with playing, competing, or winning.

Joy, on the other hand, depends on relationship— of friendship, of love, of commitment and dedication. The term "relationship," it should be noted, is to be understood as connoting an attachment of a positive sort, a connection that binds people into an emotional unity in which they are drawn to each other. It is to be distinguished from "relation," a logical term that connotes simply a way in which two things are associated. In the sentence "A hit B," the relation *hit* associates A and B, but it does not connect them. When two people are married, they should be involved in a *relationship*, but if they hate each other, they are legally related, but it can fairly be said that they have no *relationship*, only a *relation*. Joy is a form of satisfaction root-ed in a relationship in which each assumes an indispensable, and perhaps the principal, role for the other. It is the experience of gratification that flows from the awareness and appreciation of the value of the other and hence of the relationship.

II

Relationship is particularly important as a source of joy in the religious experience. The biblical verse "You shall rejoice before the Lord Your God" means that we are to rejoice, not merely because of the subjectively pleasant satisfaction derived from being in His presence, but because of our relationship with Him. It appears as a requirement in all relationships with the Supreme Being. "You shall rejoice before the Lord Your God"[1] is a command prescribing the posture that a Jew should adopt when he visits the Holy Temple during the major festi-vals. When engaging in prayer, he is instructed to "serve the Lord with joy."[2] When responding to the will of God, he is encouraged to experience "the joy of the *mitzvah*."[3] When he brings his first fruits to Jerusalem, he is told, "You shall rejoice with all the good that the Lord your God has given you and your household."[4] The experience of joy, attained when the Holy Temple in Jerusalem was the center of Jewish religious life, was realized through the offering of sacrifices—which entailed, not the eating of sacrificial meat to appease hunger, but by its means to be involved with the Supreme Being.

In the talmudic perspective, joy is so clearly independent of subjective personal gratification that it is regarded as mandato-

---

[1] Deuteronomy 16:11.
[2] Psalms 100:2.
[3] The phrase occurs frequently in the Talmud; among other places, in Shabbat 30b.
[4] Deuteronomy 26:11.

ry even in circumstances of tragedy and grief. The Mishnah
declares, "A person is obligated to bless God when he suffers
from evil just as he blesses God when he is the recipient of
good."[5] In a subsequent discussion, the Talmud declares that
"to bless God" means "to accept frustrating circumstances with
joy."[6] It is possible to do so only if the afflicted individual is
preoccupied primarily with his relationship with the Supreme
Being—rather than with the gratification of his physical
impulses or aesthetic inclinations—and if the satisfaction that
he derives from the relationship is so intense that it eclipses his
physical pain and emotional suffering. The prophet Habakkuk
expressed it in dramatic terms:

> For though the fig tree shall not blossom; neither shall
> fruit be found in the vines; the labor of the olive shall fail,
> and the fields shall yield no food; the flock shall be cut off
> from the fold, and there shall be no herd in the stalls; yet
> will I rejoice in the Lord; I will rejoice in the God of my
> salvation.[7]

The primary importance of relation with God is conveyed
implicitly by the manner in which the people of Israel in the
desert were punished when they allowed themselves to be
demoralized following the depressing report of the spies.
Moses pleaded for forgiveness, and God responded affirma-
tively. Then He pronounced the sentence: every member of that
generation would die in the desert, none would enter the Holy
Land save Joshua and Caleb. This raises an obvious question: if
indeed God forgave, why the punishment? The answer is that
His forgiveness implied a restoration of the people's relationship with Him, and this was the more important consideration.

---

[5] Berachot 54a.
[6] Ibid. 60b.
[7] Habakkuk 3:17–18.

Punishment in the form of the trial and tribulation of life in the desert was not Moses' major preoccupation.

A blessing usually begins with the formula "Blessed art Thou, Lord our God, King of the universe." According to one sage in the Jerusalem Talmud, a very important component in this formula, in addition to the one that mentions God's name or that He is sovereign of the universe (the only requirements mandated according to the Babylonian Talmud),[8] is the one that addresses Him as *atah*, "Thou."[9] The reason for this is that the word "Thou" can only be used when God is perceived as present and can be directly addressed, that is, only when one can be involved with Him in a relationship. It cannot be used when He is contemplated as removed from the speaker, in which case He can be spoken about only as "He," that is, in the third person. To affirm that He is God and that He rules the universe is to refer to Him in the third person; it is to imagine Him as distant and beyond our capacity to involve ourselves with Him in a direct relationship. According to the opinion offered in the Jerusalem Talmud, the word *atah* in the blessing declares a personal relationship, and that is of crucial importance; it is an indispensable prerequisite to joy.

Accordingly, if a person afflicted with tragedy turns away from God, he thinks of Him only in the third person. He may question Him, challenge Him, or even reject Him. He is distressed, filled with sadness and frustration. If, in such circumstances, he turns toward God, addressing Him in the second person—and this is the response of one who under all conditions seeks relationship with God—he will experience a sense of well-being despite the tragedy; he will be comforted, uplifted, and feel a sense of joy. According to the opinion cited in the Jerusalem Talmud, therefore, a crucial part of a blessing is the element by which we express the fact that we turn toward Him

---

[8] Berachot 12a.
[9] Jerusalem Talmud, Berachot 9:1, beginning.

rather than away from Him, that is, we address Him as "Thou." By doing so, we affirm that we rejoice in our relationship with Him, and this even in circumstances of pain and suffering.

Martin Buber introduced the I-Thou relationship as the fundamental category in philosophic discourse. He argued that it is the I-Thou relation rather than the I-It that is basic to human existence and human interaction. To refer to someone as an "It" is to contemplate him in the third person and as removed from the speaker; to speak of him as "Thou" is to perceive him as present and as involved with the speaker.[10] It is the gratifying experience of relationship, according to halachic thought, that is prerequisite to joy.

III

Relationships in human interaction are also essential to joy. The *halachah* emphasizes this in a variety of contexts. Rejoicing during a festival requires it. Maimonides is explicit on this score. He writes in connection with the obligation to rejoice on the festivals:

> And when he eats and drinks, he is obligated to arrange for the stranger, the orphan, and the widow together with other poor to eat. But he who locks the door of his courtyard, and eats and drinks with his children and his wife, and does not provide for the poor and those of bitter heart, is not experiencing the joy of the *mitzvah* but the pleasure of the stomach.[11]

The Torah is quite explicit in requiring a pilgrimage to Jerusalem during the three major festivals in order to provide the pilgrim with the opportunity to "rejoice in the presence of

---

[10] *I and Thou* (New York: Scribner's), pp. 2–5.
[11] *Mishneh Torah*, Hilchot Yom Tov 6:18.

the Lord your God." In addition, this joy is to be expressed by
way of partaking of a peace offering of joy. The joy of this *mitzvah*, even during the physical act of the consumption of food, is
to be based, not merely on family relationships but also on relationships with God and fellow Jews. The pleasures of the stom-
ach consist merely in the satisfaction of hunger.

Joy is an essential and defining characteristic of the Jewish
wedding. The last two of the *sheva brachot*, the seven blessings
recited under the marriage canopy, focus upon it. These blessings petition the Almighty to bring joy to the beloved friends,
namely, the bride and groom, and pay tribute to Him who created exultation and rejoicing. The potential for genuine joy, a
consequence of the new relationship created by the act of marriage, is enormous, and thus these blessings. Joy accordingly is
found in relationships of interpersonal experiences, especially
in the context of marriage. Indeed, it is the institution of marriage that provides the possibility of intensive and in-depth
relationship, and therefore of joy *par excellence*.

A similar conclusion may be drawn from the laws of mourning. Certain forms of gratification are prohibited during the
period of mourning. Most of them are identical to those proscribed on the day of *Yom Kippur*, all of which are applications
of the biblical principle *ve'initem et nafshoteichem*, "you shall
afflict your souls."[12] On both occasions, we are to refrain from
bathing, deny ourselves comfortable leather shoes, and avoid
conjugal relations. But there is a fundamental difference
between the two. During mourning, the obligation is to experience sadness and a sense of loss. On the Day of Atonement, the
imperative is to experience joy. The Day of Atonement is a day
of *simchah*, joy. As in the case of all other festival days, if a family is in mourning and *Yom Kippur* arrives, the *shivah* period of
mourning is suspended. A day of public rejoicing nullifies a
period of private mourning, with which it is incompatible. All

---

[12] Leviticus 23:27.

must partake of the joy of a public festival day. During a period of mourning, on the other hand, boundaries are set to the
experience of joy. While the elimination of all relationships—
whether with God or with family members—is neither feasible
nor desirable, the mourner is prohibited from attending din-
ners and parties, which provide opportunities to engage others
in gratifying relations, in which joy is experienced in intensive
form. It is relationship—with God and with human beings—
that is the source of joy.

IV

The dependence of joy on relationship requires further elaboration. It has been noted that pleasures can also be experienced in the context of relationships, for example, in sports. We
have observed, however, that if a player seeks the satisfactions
of playing, or of competition, or of victory, the emotion that he
is anticipating is pleasure, not joy. The reason for the absence of
joy in these circumstances is that pleasure is essentially an egoistical state of affairs, as distinguished from joy, which is fun-
damentally altruistic. If I play with someone and I seek my satisfaction, I experience pleasure. Should I be concerned, as well,
with the satisfaction of my opponent in the game, I am open to
the possibility of joy. Joy is a concomitant of selflessness or
unselfishness.

Some people are rational egoists, that is, they practice a selfish variety of unselfishness. They may be prepared to forgo the
pleasures of the moment and behave altruistically in the interests of enjoying larger and longer-lasting pleasures in the
future. They then reveal themselves to be rational, not
unselfish, in the pursuit of pleasure, and their preoccupation
remains the appropriation of subjective satisfactions, namely,
pleasure.

Rabbi Joseph B. Soloveitchik distinguished between Adam I
and Adam II in his classic essay *The Lonely Man of Faith*. Adam

I seeks success and control in the enterprises of life. Adam II pursues relationship with the Supreme Being in what Rabbi Soloveitchik designates the covenantal community. Adam I is motivated by considerations of self-interest. By being creative and exercising control in a social context, he builds institutions—hospitals, schools, and so on—that serve the community. Still, he seeks ego satisfaction in the form of achievement and deference from the community whose life his efforts have enhanced. To that extent, he experiences pleasure rather than joy. Adam II, on the other hand, finds fulfillment in the genuine and sincere service of God, with Whom he seeks relationship, and in Whom he finds redemption. When he, in the spirit of dedication, renders services of benefit to the community, his motivation is not honor and applause, but responding to divine imperatives. A concomitant of such activity is joy.

There is the pleasure of giving and the joy of giving. If responding to the needs of the poor prompts satisfaction because the donor, in comparing himself to the recipient, sees himself as in a more fortunate position, his feeling will be that of pleasure. If, on the other hand, he perceives his generous gesture to be obligatory and derives satisfaction from the opportunity to engage in a relationship with one who is oppressed, he experiences joy.

Another way of formulating this distinction is by noting that pleasure is dependent on the satisfaction of needs, whereas joy arises out of the appropriation of value. The concept of value needs to be delineated. Some equate values with needs; they hold that whatever satisfies a need is a value. According to this interpretation, when an individual pursues the satisfaction of his own needs, he is preoccupied with the realization of value. There is, then, no incompatibility between engaging in self-interested activity and the pursuit of value; indeed they can be regarded as synonymous. For Judaism, it is otherwise; in fact, quite the opposite. A value to an individual is that which he judges to be of self-transcending importance. A value is experienced when something or someone beyond oneself is judged to possess intrinsic worth. When one finds gratification in his involvement with that which possesses value, he experiences joy rather than pleasure. If, on the other hand, a person adopts a self-interested perspective, that is, if he is preoccupied with himself alone, if he finds nothing sufficiently important in an intrinsic way with the one with whom he might enter into a relationship, then he is capable of experiencing pleasures, but he is a stranger to joy.

Love, if it is genuine and therefore disinterested, inspires joy because of the value the lover attaches to his beloved. One experiences surpassing joy when the object of one's love is Infinite and of Supreme value. Accordingly, a religiously minded Jew rejoices in his relationship with God because of the satisfaction he derives from the knowledge that he is involved with the One Whom he believes to be of Eternal and Infinite Value. An identical experience is available to those whose performance of a *mitzvah* is prompted by the recognition that it is commanded by the Supreme Being and hence of unlimited value.

It is significant that the fulfillment of the biblical imperative *vesumachta bechagecha*, "you shall rejoice on the festival," required a *korban*, or sacrifice, in the form of *shalmei simchah*, peace offerings of joy. It was a sacrifice shared by the altar, which consumed designated portions of the animal, the priests, and the donor. Its purpose was to instill joy into the celebration of the festival. The implication of associating the obligation to rejoice with a sacrificial offering is that there is no joy without sacrifice, without giving, without dedication.

There is an interesting genre of religious literature designed to give an account of the *taamei hamitzvot*, the reasons for the commandments. Explanations are offered that seek to justify the commandments in human terms by explaining how their observance advances well-being in the human community.[13] One such explanation has its source in the Midrash. It declares, *lo nitnu hamitsvot elah letzaref et habriot*,[14] "the commandments were given only to connect human beings." Genuine connections leading to well-being can be achieved only if the connection is a manifestation of commitment. The sages recognized the variety of relationships into which an individual can enter and the differences among them. On the phrase in the *Ethics of the Fathers*, "Acquire a friend,"[15] Maimonides distinguishes between the *ohev to-elet*, the self-interested lover, as in the case of business partners who enter into a relationship motivated by profit, and the *ohev maalah*, the lover of virtue. The latter and his beloved together seek to help each other in achieving moral and spiritual growth for both of them. The *ohev to-eles* is

---

[13] Some rabbinic commentators refuse to engage in this variety of rationalization. They argue that the attempt to penetrate the mind of the Supreme Being is futile because it is beyond the human capacity to do so. Those who, like Maimonides, dwell on the reasons for the divine precepts do not deny that the primary motivation to abide by the commandments is that they are expressions of the Divine Will. But their pursuit of this enterprise of rationalization is a way of asserting that, while other inscrutable reasons may have been the divine purpose in commanding the *mitzvot*, it is nevertheless also God's will and intent to enhance man's well-being and bring joy into the lives of individuals and the community. On the other hand, those who decline to discuss the reasons for the commandments do not deny that a primary objective of Torah is to bring joy and well-being into the life of man. There are biblical passages in abundance that promise a life of blessing in the world here and now if man will but undertake to live by the divine imperatives. They merely refuse to contemplate that which is universally agreed to be inscrutable.

[14] *Genesis Rabbah* 44. It may be noted that the interpretation of the clause cited here is not the only one and may not even be the one preferred by commentators, but it does have the advantage of directing attention to the fact that human well-being is a function of interrelationships.

[15] Avot 1:6.

prompted by selfish objectives, the *ohev maalah* is moved by altruistic considerations. It is the latter type of relationship that translates into joy and a sense of well-being.

Joy and pleasure can easily be equated because they often occur in tandem, in the performance of identical acts. In the last analysis, which of these two emotions a person experiences will depend on his motivation. An incentive for an act of love may be a genuine appreciation of the beloved and a commitment to the beloved's welfare, in which case the emotion experienced would be one of joy. If, on the other hand, this act were prompted by a desire to satisfy biological impulses, the experience would simply be one of pleasure. One of the differences between what the Talmud refers to as love with an ulterior motive and love that is sincere and genuine is that the exercise of the former leads only to pleasure, while the latter will experience joy as well.

Marriage offers an opportunity for both the satisfaction of needs and the realization of values. The personal comforts and the gratification of organic impulses that contribute significantly to well-being are obviously essential in the marital relationship. But even more important is the joy that arises from the unselfish and disinterested love for another human being and the possibility of building a family, an object of love, in accordance with cherished values of Torah. A person who perceives marriage as merely a context for the pursuit of pleasure deprives himself of the opportunity to enrich his life with something of enormously greater value, namely, the experience of joy.

A similar analysis is appropriate to the relationship of man to the Divine Being. If religious observance is prodded by the consideration that it will be accompanied by reciprocal rewards, then assuming this in fact happens, it will result in the experience of pleasure. It is the approach of the rational egoist. If, on the other hand, religious observance is based on selfless commitment, it will be accompanied by joy. In the case of the love of God, the experience of joy may, at least among the deeply religious, become so intense that it could appropriately be described as ecstasy.

V

We have concluded thus far that joy, unlike egoistical pleasure, presupposes a relationship in which an individual perceives another—a human being, the Divine Being, or even a cause—as possessing extraordinary value. It is the appropriation and appreciation of this value that is the basis of the experience of joy.

It should be noted at this point that it is not easy for an individual who has devoted his life to the pursuit of pleasure, and who is invariably guided by considerations of self-interest, to acknowledge the existence of joy as an experience distinct from pleasure and to appreciate its value. He is like a person born blind, who cannot even imagine what color is like because he has never experienced it. Those who do not allow themselves to enter into genuine relationships and to experience the value they make available are incapable of imagining joy and appreciating its worth. A consideration of the implications of the attitudes that lie at the basis of joy will hint at its nature and reveal the superiority of joy over pleasure.

Pleasure is a lonely state; joy excludes loneliness because, by definition, it involves relationships—between man and God, between man and society, and between man and man. The pleasure-seeker may experience loneliness even when surrounded by multitudes, for example, in a densely populated city, because he is foreign to relationships. The one who treasures joy will not suffer this disability even in a village if it is a place where relationships are encouraged. As a matter of fact, the pleasure-seeker will be inclined to live in a city precisely because it maximizes opportunities for pleasure. The person who values joy will seek community, which he could easily

find even in a village. The superiority of community to loneliness is pointedly expressed in Ecclesiastes: "Two are better
than one. . . . If two sleep together, they keep warm, but how
can one keep warm alone?"[16]

Further, joy, unlike pleasure, is a sign that life has been
expanded and enhanced. The experience of joy, because it
requires relationship, presupposes a distinctive variety of unity
of at least two persons. This unity is highly significant because
it is not prompted by pragmatic, self-interested considerations.
The unity at the basis of joy is inspired by an urge to become
permanently attached, to share a life, to merge with another. It
is a unity in which, in a real sense, each appropriates into his
life the life of the other. It is most frequently exemplified in the
relation of marriage. When a mate passes away, the surviving
spouse experiences a sudden emptiness and often declares that
life has, in significant measure, been robbed of meaning. There
is a unity that is profitable; two people can develop a relationship of friendship on the basis of self-interested considerations.
Such a unity yields pleasure. There is a unity that is meaningful; it is productive of joy. It is the latter that enriches life.

The relation of a Jew to the people of Israel should involve
this type of unity. It ought not to be merely a unity of self-interest in which, for example, Jews combine to defend themselves
against the onslaught of anti-Semitism, and in which there is a
personal advantage for each. It should be the kind of unity in
which Jews are tied to each other by bonds of love and commitment, a unity which transforms a collection of individual
Jews into an organic unity. Jewish sages have emphasized the
importance of this relation, and Jews, in their conduct, often
exemplify it. More than any other community, if a tragedy
occurs within a Jewish family or community, the pain is widespread.

---

[16] Ecclesiastes 9:11.

It is this kind of unity that should characterize the Jew's relation to God. The halachic Jew experiences it in the form of love. The religious Jew who has adopted a mystical posture seeks to transcend love and to achieve a unity that may be described as one of cleaving to the Divine Being. In either case, such varieties of unity bring joy to their participants.

Chapter 9

Truth

Truth has both a cognitive and a moral dimension; we shall be concerned with the latter. There are two types of action associated with truth, and each raises issues of a moral character. One is seeking truth; its goal is the possession of truth. The formulation of truths is a perennial occupation of man and, of course, the main concern of science. There are two questions that need to be considered with respect to our search for truth. First, is there an obligation to seek it? Second, are we obligated to take into account the human consequences of the search, or may we pursue it without giving any consideration to its human ramifications on the grounds that the possession of truth contains intrinsic and unconditional value?

The other type of activity related to truth is speaking the truth. Assertions for which truth is claimed may be used to instruct, to teach, or to guide. This poses a moral question: is it always necessary to tell the truth, the whole truth, and nothing but the truth, or are there situations in which one is justified in deviating from the truth? This question presupposes yet another, nonmoral issue: is it even possible to tell the whole truth and nothing but the truth?

A fundamental problem underlies all discussions of truth as a moral ideal: Are all values equally commanding, or are some

superior to others, that is, are there circumstances in which, for
moral reasons, one is required to stray from the truth—either
the search or the articulation? If the latter, where is truth to be
located in the hierarchy?

I

The starting point of this discussion is the question whether
there is a moral or ethical obligation to pursue the truth? The
acquisition of truth, when considered apart from its implications for human welfare, is certainly a cognitive ideal. It is also,
according to a celebrated ancient Greek philosopher, an ethical
ideal. No pleasure, he teaches, is as intense and as valuable as
is that which accompanies the possession of knowledge.
Knowledge is a distinctively human achievement. The acquisition of theoretical truths concerning man and the universe
enables the human being to function in a manner that is
supremely human and, for that reason, has as its concomitant
the highest form of pleasure. It accordingly becomes an ethical
objective of the highest order to amass knowledge.

It should be noted that there exists a powerful, irresistible
urge to acquire truths. It is for many almost a dogma of faith
that truth is invariably of positive value. Whenever scientists
make a significant discovery, it is almost universally greeted
with great joy in the scientific community. Even when they recognize the potentially devastating consequences of what they
have acquired, they cannot refrain from pursuing the enterprise. Scientists fully understood the implications of the formula that translated matter into energy, which, when turned
into technology, resulted in the destruction of vast populations,
but they revealed their discovery nevertheless. It could be
argued that they did so because of the exigencies of World War
II and the need to defeat the enemy. It could be maintained,
however, that there is a relentless inner dynamic that prompts

scientists ever to press onward in the search for truth. When new methods of biotechnology were introduced, the question was raised whether the secrets revealed should be made available to mankind in view of the harmful consequences that might ensue. The question received the anticipated affirmative reply.

Is truth, in Jewish thought, an ideal to be pursued irrespective of any ulterior considerations? According to Maimonides, there exists an obligation to know the truth about God. He writes:

> The fundamental principle of all and the pillar of all wisdom is to know that there is a First Being Who brings all other beings into existence. . . . And this knowledge is a positive commandment, for it is written "I am the Lord your God."[1]

The failure to entertain certain fundamental truths about God, according to Maimonides, brands one a heretic. He writes:

> Five are called *minim* [nonbelievers]: he who says that there is no God and that the world has no guide; he who says that the world has a guide but that they are two or more; he who says that there exists one Master but that He has a form or image; and also the one who says that He is not alone the first and the creator of all; and also the one who worships a star or a constellation as an intermediary between himself and the Master of the universe. Three are called *apikursim* [misbelievers]: he who denies prophecy and maintains that there is no knowledge that emanates from God and reaches the heart of man; he who

---

[1] *Mishneh Torah*, Hilchot Yesodei Hatorah 1:1.

denies the prophecy of Moses our teacher; and he who claims that God does not know the actions of men.[2]

The possession of truth about that which is ultimate in the universe is clearly a condition *sine qua non* for the good life and a fundamental obligation for mankind. But further, it could be maintained convincingly that any truths that enable one to proceed by reasoned analysis to the knowledge of ultimate truths are also included under the obligation to know God. The arguments that Maimonides uses to prove the existence of God in the *Guide to the Perplexed* are identified in philosophic literature as cosmological and teleological. Both these types of argument begin with premises that formulate principles of knowledge concerning the physical universe. Such knowledge, it can be argued, is also included in the obligation to know God.

It is true that not all Jewish thinkers agree that the knowledge of God is an ultimate value. For many, it is sufficient to *believe* that God exists and that He presented the people of Israel with the Torah. They appear to maintain that the fundamental principle of halachic Judaism is not truth but obligation—in other words, *mitzvot*. It has already been noted that Rabbi Abraham Ibn Daud (Ravad), in a commentary on the Maimonidean dictum that he who believes that God possesses a form and image is a heretic, declared that truth is not always a value to be pursued. Even if one entertains errors concerning the nature of God, he may still be counted among the righteous and the pious, and of a spiritual standing greater than even Maimonides, because the fundamental value is not understanding of God but responding to the will of God, that is, the study and fulfillment of the obligations of Torah. The view of the Ravad is related to the question of the priority of values. It may be that the search for truth stands lower on the hierarchy

---

[2] Ibid., Hilchot Teshuvah 3:7–8.

of values, and must accept a subordinate and less significant status, than obedience to obligation.

But there are truths that are unrelated to the pursuit of the knowledge of God. These involve generalizations concerning the physical universe that are useful because of the technological miracles into which they can be translated. Is there an obligation to pursue the acquisition of such truths irrespective of their practical utility? By way of response, it should be noted, in the first place, that such truths, which are often labeled scientific laws, in fact receive two interpretations. According to one, they describe relations that are exemplified in the universe; they in fact reveal the structure of things. If the objection is raised that generalizations thought to have been verified have too often turned out not to be accurate, it is countered by an admission that the criticism is valid and the claim that with the passing of time, science will get closer and closer to truths that express the structure of things, that science is in fact approaching that structure asymptotically. The other interpretation has it that the laws formulated in theoretical physics are the creative and imaginative inventions of scientists, and, notwithstanding, that they are useful for predicting and explaining the course of natural events. On this view, no claim is made that the laws reflect inherent relations. They are true but only in a pragmatic sense, that is, they work.

Rabbi Joseph B. Soloveitchik adopts the latter view concerning the nature of scientific truths; he regards them as possessing essentially instrumental value. As he puts it

> In his full resplendent glory and as a creative agent of God, he [the theoretical physicist] constructs his own world and in a mysterious fashion succeeds in controlling his environment through manipulating his own mathematical constructs and creations.[3]

---

[3] In Studies in Judaica, ed. Leon Stitskin (New York: Ktav, 1974), p. 78.

Objective truth, therefore, cannot be claimed for the theoretical scientist's formulations, and they are at best of instrumental significance, that is, they are pragmatically true. Hence when Rabbi Soloveitchik argued in favor of the view that there is an obligation to seek knowledge of the material and physical worlds, he did so on practical, pragmatic grounds. In his *The Lonely Man of Faith*, he distinguished between Adam I, who seeks control in the universe by imitating God in his creative activity, and Adam II, who seeks redemption through relationship with God. Adam I is motivated by the biblical imperative *vechibshuha*—conquer the universe. The outstanding paradigm of Adam I is the theoretical physicist, whose formulations are translated into technological accomplishments for the benefit of mankind.[4] According to Rabbi Soloveitchik, therefore, there is an obligation to seek and to gain knowledge concerning the physical universe, though because of its instrumental, not its inherent, value—it serves the needs of man.

There are accordingly two varieties of truth with respect to which the question as to whether we are obligated to know them arises. One may be called metaphysical or, better still, theological truth. Such truths, espoused in the age of Maimonides, include propositions concerning the existence and nature of God and any assertions about the physical universe from which conclusions may be deduced concerning the existence and nature of God. Whether the obligation to know such truths is ultimate and unconditional or subordinate to obligations that are more commanding is debated in rabbinic literature. Clearly, even with respect to that which is fundamental in the theological enterprise, namely, knowledge of the attributes and actions of God, truth need not be of supreme importance. Certainly it is not according to Ravad. The other variety of truth focuses on the physical universe. These are truths which are irrelevant to

---

[4] Ibid., pp. 76–79.

theological claims and are intended primarily to reveal relations that inhere in nature. Concerning the latter, it can be argued, as Rabbi Soloveitchik does, that they are essentially of a pragmatic nature and of instrumental value. Such knowledge derives its value from the fact that it contributes to human well-being in either an aesthetic or a technological mode. If it fails to do so, its pursuit can be avoided. If it were ascertained that a proposition whose truth scientists seek to establish is a threat to human well-being, the enterprise need not be advanced.

II

Clearly, there exists a moral obligation to speak the truth. This is especially the case in testifying in a courtroom. The Talmud declares that judges have the obligation to examine a witness's testimony with three categories of questions, all intended to elicit the truth. But is it really possible to speak the truth at all times? More significantly, assuming that it is, are there circumstances in which one may deviate from the truth?

It is noteworthy that when a witness takes an oath in an American courtroom, he is required to swear that he will speak the truth, the whole truth, and nothing but the truth. The reasons for utilizing this formula are obvious. First of all, a witness should make every effort to ensure that his declarations are true. It is possible that he may omit information of which he has knowledge that seriously reflects on the case, and this too is a distortion; hence, he must affirm that he is telling the whole truth. It is also possible for him to interpret his declaration that he shall speak the truth as meaning that among his assertions, some will be only approximately true; hence he must add the phrase "and nothing but the truth," to exclude such an escape from truth. But there is a more fundamental question that needs to be raised: is it really possible to speak the whole truth and nothing but the truth?

The obligation to speak truly is commanded in the Torah in the phrase "Remove yourself from falsehood." Why did the Torah not formulate this obligation in a positive form, namely, "Speak the truth"? One answer might be that it is impossible always to speak truthfully, and that the most that can be required of a less than perfect human being is that he remove himself from falsehood as much as possible.

A biblical passage with its rabbinic commentary provides an immediate illustration. "Moses said, Thus said the Lord, at about midnight, I shall go among the Egyptians, and the first-born of the Egyptians will die." Noting the use of the word "about," which connotes uncertainty, the Talmud comments:

> Did God indeed state "about midnight"; is there doubt with the Almighty? Rather God said "at midnight," but Moses repeated what He said in the words "At about midnight" . . . because the star gazers of Pharaoh might err and say "Moses is a liar."[5]

Because of the possible miscalculations of the stargazers, who might think that the death of the firstborn began past midnight or before it and thus would attribute falsehood to the Divine Being, Moses decided to fudge the precise statement that God made to him. In many circumstances, truth is hard to find.

Science is very much aware of this. The more precise the assertion, the more uncertain is its truth. A statement such as "The water is hot" is easily determined to be true if it is interpreted to mean hot to the touch. The statement "The water is 180 degrees Fahrenheit" is more difficult to verify. The thermometer may read 180 degrees, but it may be afflicted with a margin of error. The true temperature may be 179.9 degrees or

---

[5] Berachot 3b.

180.1 degrees, in which case the assertion that it is 180 degrees is false.

But it is not only the requirement of precision that frustrates the scientific resolve to arrive at truth; the very attempt to formulate generalizations is beset by numerous obstacles which render doubtful the claim that scientific propositions are true, and this is so especially when they belong to theories of science. The theory of gravity, for example, held to be absolute since Newton's time, was finally discovered to be false,[6] and was replaced by Einstein's theory of relativity. The tendency of scientists to assume that their discoveries constitute revelations of the universe's inherent structure was seriously shaken. Now they speak with greater humility and suggest that their generalizations may be theoretical constructions—inventions of the human mind that seem to work but do not necessarily reflect precisely the inherent structure of the universe. They also argue that their generalizations are essentially of pragmatic significance and thus do not claim that in formulating laws of nature they are describing relations that are exemplified in the universe. Truths concerning nature are difficult to come by, and we cannot be certain that laws of science that are ostensibly verified are in fact true. So the Torah does not require that we shall at all times speak the truth; our obligation is rather that we shall, as much as is possible, withdraw from falsehood.

But this biblical imperative has another meaning which is based on the fact that there are occasions when we may stray from truth or perhaps may even be obligated to do so. The following discussion appears in the Talmud:

Rabbi Ila'ah said in the name of Rabbi Elazar son of Rabbi Shimon: A man is permitted to deviate from truth for the

---

[6] Cf. Thomas S. Kuhn, *The Structure of Scientific Revolutions* (University of Chicago Press, 1996), ch. IX.

sake of peace, for it is written: "Your father instructed us before his death as follows: So shall you say to Joseph: 'Pray forgive the transgression of your brothers and their sin, for they dealt with you in an evil manner' " [Rashi explains that Jacob never asked them to do so]. Rabbi Nathan said that it is an obligation, for it is written [when God asked Samuel to anoint another as king in the place of Saul], "And Samuel said, How can I go, and Saul will hear of it and he will kill me" (I Samuel 16:2). And God said, "Take a calf in your hand and say that you have come to sacrifice to the Lord" [i.e., God told him to deviate from truth]. In the school of Rabbi Yishmael it was taught: Even God deviates from the truth. First, it is written, when Sarah was informed that in her old age she would give birth to a son, "And Sarah laughed in her heart, saying, After I am old will I have pleasure and my master is old," but later [when God reported this to Abraham], God said, "Why did Sarah laugh, saying, 'Will I truly give birth and I am old?' " (Genesis 18:12–13). [Rashi adds that God deviated from truth to preserve peace between Abraham and Sarah].[6]

It would appear that the ideal of preserving peace often takes priority over truth, and the latter may be modified if necessary for the sake of harmonious relations. But there are other values that take priority. "Rabbi Yehudah said in the name of Samuel: In these three things may a person digress from truth: with regard to a tractate, to cohabitation, and to hospitality." Rashi explains. If someone asks a scholar whether he knows a certain tractate of the Talmud, he is to say no even though he does in fact know it, for "this is the virtue of humility"; if someone asks a question dealing with relations of intimacy, he is to deny the occurrence of an event that actually took place, and

---

[7] Yevamot 65b.

"this is the virtue of modesty"; if someone asks whether a certain individual whose hospitality he enjoyed is a good host, he should not give him a rave review even if it is deserved, and this is a virtue, for otherwise others will impose upon the host and impoverish him. The last may be interpreted as required by the virtue of human sensitivity.[7]

In any case, what is abundantly clear is that the values of peace, humility, modesty, and sensitivity often take precedence over truth. Truth concerning factual empirical matters affecting human well-being is not an absolute value. It does have intrinsic value, for it is better to live with truth than falsehood, but primarily its value is instrumental. If in speaking the truth we can serve the cause of compassion, justice, and peace, and if we can do so in a posture of humility and modesty, it ought to be articulated; otherwise not. This is a second reason for the biblical formulation of the command with respect to articulating truth in the negative, namely, "withdraw from falsehood," rather that the positive "Thou shalt always speak the truth." There are occasions when, to secure superior values, it may be necessary to deviate from truth; otherwise refrain from falsehood, and at all times get as close to truth as possible.

It is important to stress this point because there are theories of morality that require speaking the truth at all times without exception, irrespective of consequences to others. Such, for example, is the deontological theory of Immanuel Kant. Whatever is required by the categorical imperative must be fulfilled unconditionally. Speaking truly is one such requirement.[8] Judaism does not endorse this view. There are other striking examples of Judaism's subordination of truth to values assigned priority in the Jewish scheme of things. Both speaking evil of another, *leshon hara*, and slander, *motzi shem ra*, are for-

---

[8] Baba Metzia 23b.

[9] Kant, *Fundamental Principles of the Metaphysic of Morals* (New York: Liberal Arts Press, 1949), pp. 39–43.

bidden. A differences between the two is that when we commit slander we speak falsely, whereas in speaking evil we utter that which is true. The circumstance that what is said is true does not justify speaking evil. Another illustration, which emerges out of the requirement of humility, is, according to Nachmanides, that we shall always perceive another as greater than we are. But clearly, this cannot always reflect truth. A pious sage is obviously superior to an immoral ignoramus. But it is not the truth that is controlling in this matter, but humility. The humble man always treats others *as if* they are superior, though this may obviously not be the case.

There are occasions when the obligation to speak the truth is not nullified but enhanced by other moral principles. This occurs, for example, when a witness testifies in a courtroom. He may hesitate to do so on the grounds that he may harm the defendant, with whom he may be involved in a relation of friendship. But the requirements of justice, in addition to truth, demand that he do so.

III

The discussion leads to another and fundamental problem. What is the location of truth on the scale of moral values? It is necessary to identify its position if we are to determine in each instance the extent to which it is mandatory to speak the truth. The scale is not explicitly delineated in biblical and rabbinic sources; it must somehow be deduced from the cases upon which the Talmud and its commentaries elaborate. A few insights may perhaps be revealing.

There is a moral challenge and a moral problem. The moral challenge arises when an impulse to commit a moral transgression confronts a moral principle that prohibits it. Under these circumstances, the appropriate response is to exhibit strength of resolve and resist the temptation. The moral problem occurs when two moral principles require contradictory responses to an action one is about to undertake, in which case the primary task is to determine which of the two is to be assigned priority. A patient asks his physician whether his illness is fatal. Is the physician obligated to speak the truth, or may he, in the spirit of compassion, assure his patient that it is not and allay his patient's anxieties?

The relationship among moral values is not linear, which is to say that moral values cannot be located on a vertical line in such a way that those on its lower portions will always be subordinate to those above them. The reason for this is that the value to be assigned priority will also depend on circumstances, so that, as between two values, A and B, in one set of conditions, A will be given greater importance than B, and in other circumstances, the reverse will be the case. By way of illustration, consider two values other than truth, namely, justice and compassion. In the courtroom, justice is invariably supreme, and little room is allowed for compassion. "Do not favor persons in judgment, you shall listen to the big man and the small man equally,"[9] upon which Rashi comments:

> You [i.e., the judge] shall not say, "This man is poor and his adversary is wealthy, and he has an obligation to help the poor man, I shall judge in favor of the poor man."

A judge may not, accordingly show favor to an indigent person as a matter of compassion; justice is indifferent to poverty and wealth. If, however, a rich man finds an object which has no distinguishing marks and thus he may legally claim it as his own, he is encouraged to return it if he knows who lost it. This is the meaning of *lifnim m'shurat hadin*, "going beyond the requirements of the law," a general concept which in this specific application requires the display of compassion rather than

---

[10] Deuteronomy 1:17.

the application of the rule of justice, which declares that if an object that was found has no telltale marks by which ownership can be determined, it belongs to the one who found it.

The implication is that the task of deciding which values do, in fact, enjoy priority in any context is intricate. It involves an ability to judge the relative importance of values in the light of the circumstances in relation to which judgment is sought. The relationship among moral values, therefore, is not linear but takes the form of a structure consisting of many vertical lines, each one of which is lodged in a state of affairs, and in such a way that a specific value may occur at diverse locations on the variety of different lines.

IV

Truth may be an absolute and supreme value, certainly for thinkers such as Maimonides, when its object is the Divine Being. Not all rabbinic sages, Ravad for example, share this view. But insofar as the empirical world of human experience is concerned, however, the ideal of truth does not occupy the highest rung and should be perceived as often giving way to other ideals of greater importance, such as mercy, justice, and peace.

Chapter 10

Humility

Judaism requires humility on both religious and human grounds. It is a necessary ingredient in the religious perspective and is indispensable in social relations. The importance assigned to this character trait is considerable. In the Torah—the written and the oral—humility is associated prominently with Judaism's most outstanding representatives. No one was ever as humble as Moses.[1] One must strive to be as humble as Hillel.[2] Rabbi Judah the Prince, redactor of the Mishnah, was so proficient in this virtue that, by comparison, none of his survivors were regarded as humble. As the Talmud put it, "When Rebbe [Rabbi Judah the Prince] died, humility disappeared."[3]

The idea of humility is rich in content and inextricably bound to other principles and precepts included in the complex system of Jewish ethics. In this chapter, its wealth of meaning will be explored, and its centrality in that system will be exhibited.

---

[1] Numbers 12:3.

[2] Shabbat 30b.

[3] Sotah 49a.

[3a] In *Sefer Hamaspik* (Jerusalem, Alpha, 1965), p. 53, Avraham ben HaRambam distinguishes between what I have designated the religious and moral conceptions of humility.

I

A careful analysis reveals two independent conceptions of humility expounded in talmudic literature: (1) The religious conception—the humble person is one who believes that his achievements and acquisitions are the result of divine benevolence rather than personal power or merit. (2) The moral conception—the humble person is one who believes that his personal achievements and acquisitions, whatever they may be, provide no grounds for the judgment that he is superior to his fellow men.

The first conception is formulated in *Sefer Mitzvot Hagadol* (known as the *Semag*) of Rabbi Moshe Jacob of Coucy. He explains the verse "Take heed lest you forget the Lord your God"[4] as a warning that "the children of Israel shall not feel pride when the Holy One, blessed be He, brings them blessings, and they shall not say that they have accumulated these blessings through their own effort and thus fail to acknowledge, because of their pride, the good which they have received from the Holy One, blessed be He."[5] Rabbeinu Yonah, on the other hand, on the verse which commands the king that "his heart be not lifted up above his brethren,"[6] declares, "We are warned in this command to remove from our souls the quality of pride and that the big man shall not behave with arrogance toward the small man, but that he shall always be of humble spirit."[7] This statement is an expression of the moral conception. Both conceptions are formulated as prohibitions against pride, but humility admits of degrees, and at its lowest, it is simply the negation of pride.

---

[4] Deuteronomy 8:11.
[5] *Sefer Mitzvot Gadol,* negative commandment 64.
[6] Deuteronomy 17:20.
[7] *Shaarei Teshuvah* 3:34.

The claim that these formulations represent two conceptions rather than one is based, first, on the fact that they are factually and logically independent. One may, in behavior, exhibit the religious attitude without the moral, and vice versa. A person may acknowledge that his attainments and possessions are the products of divine grace and display humility in relation to God and yet treat others with contempt if, in his judgment, their successes fall short of his. On the other hand, another person may not believe his attainments to be in any way superior and yet, meager though they are, may identify himself as their sole and exclusive cause—in which case he is religiously arrogant and morally humble. Both types are numerous and abundantly available to human experience.

But, second, it should be noted that humility is a relational conception, that is to say, it does not denote a *quality* that may be affirmed or denied of an individual but a *relation* into which an individual enters merely as a term. For it is evident, from the philosophic point of view, that the declaration of the humble, namely "I am unimportant," does not assert that one possesses a certain quality, as is the case, for example, with the statement "I am white." Rather does it assert a relation, in the same way as the declaration "I am tall." Tallness is not an intrinsic property of an individual. It designates a relation that obtains between the individual and some standard or some other individual. Analogously, unimportance denotes a relation to some standard or to some entity. Therefore, a humble person may assert his own unimportance either in relation to God or in comparison with man, but the meaning of unimportance differs in the two cases. In one it means dependence on God; in the other it signifies that success is no basis for the judgment of superiority. These two conceptions are independent. It should also be noted, in passing, that this relational aspect of humility makes it logically possible for a person to experience simultaneously the polar sentiments of importance and unimportance. But more on this later.

By way of further clarification, the claim that there are two conceptions of humility should not be construed as a suggestion that there are differences of opinion among the interpreters of Torah as to which of these two is an imperative of *halachah*. The dispute among the sages focuses exclusively on the question as to which of the two should be assigned primacy. Some include the prohibition on one form of arrogance among the six hundred and thirteen commandments, and some include the other in the list;[8] but none removes from his conception of the *humble personality* the element stressed by the other. Thus Nachmanides, whose emphasis coincides with that of Rabbeinu Yonah, and who maintains that the biblical root of the prohibition on arrogance deals with human relations, writes, "I will therefore explain how you shall conduct yourself as a humble man. . . . Every man shall be greater than you in your eyes. . . . In all your speaking, acting, and thinking, regard yourself as though you were in the presence of God."[9] A full characterization of the humble personality, according to Nachmanides, must therefore take into account man's relation to God.

Further, arrogance and humility, at their lowest level, are correlative notions. A person is arrogant if he regards himself as the cause of his achievements or if he believes them to be the ground of his superiority. He who avoids these attitudes is humble.

The arrogant person is intellectually in error. One who exemplifies the religious conception of arrogance may declare

---

[8] Maimonides and some others exclude both conceptions from the list of 613 commandments.

[9] *Kitvei Ramban* (Jerusalem: Mosad Harav Kook, 1963), bk. I, p. 374. While the concept of humility formulated here belongs under a heading that will be characterized in the next section of this essay, it is clear that Nachmanides regards the humble personality as exemplifying both the religious and the moral conceptions.

either "My power and the might of my hand hath gotten me this wealth"[10] or "For my righteousness the Lord hath brought me to possess this land,"[11] that is, he asserts that his achievements are due to his own power or personal merit. In the first case he errs in that he fails to recognize the Almighty as at least a partial cause of his success—a human being may plant the seeds but cannot produce rain—and even as the ultimate source of all the powers he is able to activate. In the second case, he errs in that he overemphasizes the good of which he is the source and underestimates the evil of which he is also the origin.

The morally arrogant person contends that he is better than others. This claim presupposes a standard of physical strength, material accumulation, intellectual achievement, or social status. But whatever may be the standard that impresses him as most important, the arrogant individual believes that he ranks higher on the scale than those by whom he is surrounded, and consequently that he is the better man. His error, in this case, may be rooted in any of three misconceptions. He may be mistaken in his value system. If, for example, he regards material accumulation as the highest value, he errs in the standard he selects. He may also stray from the truth in his judgment. If piety and morality should be his choice of the ultimate standard, his estimate of his own attainments in relation to those of others may not be accurate. Finally, if human life is of unlimited value, he may, if his standard is good and his judgment right, maintain "My deeds are better than his," but he is not generally justified in declaring "I am better than he." He simply has no way of estimating the value of his own life in comparison with the life of another in order to make the invidious comparison.

---

[10] Deuteronomy 8:17.
[11] Ibid. 19:4.

Two important conclusions that contribute to the understanding of the idea of humility follow from this discussion.
First, humility is a function of two things: attainments and attitudes. If a person who has lived a life filled with failures
refrains from attributing whatever meager success he has accumulated to his own competence or avoids the sentiment that he
is superior to others, his attitude, while praiseworthy, cannot
be identified as one of great humility—no matter how small the
value he assigns to himself. To be outstanding in humility, one
must first be outstanding in achievements. "Now the man
Moses was very meek, above all men that were upon the face
of the earth."[12] To match the humility of Moses, one must first
reach his greatness.

Second, a sense of humility is not the same as a psychological sense of inferiority. If a person suffers from the latter sentiment, he feels incapable and incompetent. His very feeling may
interfere with his performance. The humble person believes
himself to be, not incompetent, but unimportant. He recognizes
the successes he has achieved; he is even aware of their value;
he simply avoids attaching great importance to himself because
of these successes. When Moses declared, "Who am I that I
should go unto Pharaoh and that I should bring forth the children of Israel out of Egypt?"[13] he was expressing humility;
when he insisted, "For I am slow of speech and of a slow
tongue,"[14] he was declaring incompetence. The humble person,
notwithstanding his humility, is capable of great achievement.

II

The *beliefs* described above, however, do not exhaust the
meaning of humility. Humility is exhibited in *feeling* as well. It

---

[12] Numbers 12:3.
[13] Exodus 3:11.
[14] Ibid. 4:10.

is clear that the sentiment that should be experienced by the personality who exemplifies the religious conception of humility is gratitude. If I must credit God with my success, if I am obligated to acknowledge Him as the ultimate source of all the powers I am able to activate, then I should be grateful for all the blessings He has seen fit to bestow upon me. On the other hand, the individual who exemplifies the moral conception of humility should experience what we may call the sentiment of equality. If, no matter what his attainments may be, he is not to judge himself as superior—and, according to the definition offered in the preceding section, there is no requirement for him to assign himself a value that will reduce him to a level that is inferior—he should experience himself to be the equal of others.

These two attitudes, gratitude to God and equality in relation to man, are in fact mandatory. Maimonides declares that as part of prayer, we are obligated "to give praise and thanksgiving to the Almighty for the good that He has bestowed upon us."[15] The demand that we cultivate a sense of equality was put in the form of a suggestion in the Talmud:

> A favorite saying of the rabbis of Yavneh was: I am God's creature, and my fellow is God's creature. My work is in town and his work is in the country. I rise early for my work, and he rises early for his work. Just as he does not presume to do my work, so I do not presume to do his work. Will you say that I do much and he does little? We have learned: One may do much or one may do little, it is all one provided he directs his heart to heaven. [16]

But an examination of biblical and rabbinic declarations reveals that more is required than the sentiments that are con-

---

[15] *Mishneh Torah*, Hilchot Tefillah 1:2.
[16] Berachot 17a.

comitants of the beliefs here described. Thus the *Semag*, in elaborating upon the religious conception of humility, applauds the attitude exhibited by King David, who declared, "But I am a worm and no man,"[17] and adds that this means, "I am obligated to view myself as a worm who hides beneath the dust in shame."[18] We may also recall the patriarch's expression when he was appealing to God on behalf of the people of Sodom, "But I am dust and ashes."[19] It is characteristic of the religious personality, when contemplating or addressing deity, to regard himself as of an infinitesimal quantity, a speck of dust in a vast ocean of unlimited space, a thoroughly insignificant entity. The French philosopher Pascal expressed this well:

> Returning to himself, let man consider what he is in comparison with all existence; let him regard himself as lost in a remote corner of nature; and from the little cell in which he finds himself lodged, I mean the universe, let him estimate at their true value the earth, kingdoms, cities, and himself. What is man in the Infinite? [20]

Now this attitude seems to be the counterpart of another belief altogether, not that God is the source of all my blessings, but that in relation to God I am an infinitesimal and wholly meaningless entity.

Under the heading of the moral conception of humility, it appears that more is required than the feeling of equality. Nachmanides, for example, demands of the humble personality that he direct attention to his own failings and stress the achievements of others.

---

[17] Psalms, 22:7
[18] *Sefer Mitzvot Hagadol*, Negative commandment 64.
[19] Genesis 18:27.
[20] Blaise Pascal, *Pensées*, par 72.

Every man should be great in your eyes. If he is wise or wealthy, it is your duty to honor him. If he is poor and you are richer or wiser than he, consider that you are more guilty than he, and he more innocent than you.[21]

This posture seems to involve, not so much an objective belief as the deliberate adoption of an attitude. The humble person does not prepare a balance sheet of assets and liabilities which are evaluated and weighted in order to arrive at a total which may be compared with that of somebody else. He deliberately underscores his own weakness while emphasizing the strengths of others. He adopts an attitude that is both subjective and selfless.

We must conclude that each of the two conceptions, the religious and the moral, may be exemplified in the humble personality in various degrees. Humility is a quantitative conception. In the preceding section, attention was directed to the lowest levels at which the concept of humility may be exemplified. We are now concerned with the ultimate in humble behavior. Under the heading of the religious conception, the individual who has attained to the first level believes that God is, at the least, a partial cause of his achievements, whereas the person who has reached the highest level declares that he is totally insignificant in comparison with God. In the category of the moral, the humble personality, on the lower level, believes that his successes do not justify the judgment of superiority, while on the higher level, he is determined to demonstrate that he is inferior. Each of these beliefs is accompanied by the appropriate feelings—the feelings of gratitude and insignificance in relation to God, and the sentiments of equality and inferiority in relation to man.

---

[21] Nachmanides, op. cit.

It seems appropriate, in each of the two conceptions, to distinguish between the *anav* and the *shefal ruach*. The *anav* is
grateful and accepts the idea of equality. The *shefal ruach* goes
beyond the *anav* by insisting on his own insignificance and on
his weakness in relation to others. Maimonides directed attention to these extremes in humble behavior in the following passage: "It is not good that a man shall be humble (*anav*) alone,
but that he shall be meek (*shefal ruach*) and his spirit shall be
very low."[22]

III

The concept of humility requires further clarification. It has
been said that the humble person entertains certain beliefs and
experiences certain feelings. But in the genuinely humble personality, these must be translated into actions. How then shall
we define humility behaviorally? To what kind of actions do
these beliefs and feelings give rise?

It is not possible within the limited scope of this essay to
give an exhaustive account of all the behavioral patterns that
should be associated with the posture of humility. A few
illustrations, however, will suffice for the purpose of elucidation.

A person who is humble (*anav*) in the religious sense would,
among other things, be satisfied with his portion in the world
(*sameach bechalko*). If to God belongs the credit of human
achievement, man may not claim or demand anything he does
not possess as a matter of right. Humility then sets the boundary to human ambition in the material domain. Thus Bachya
declares that one who is humble "should be contented with
whatever means of livelihood present themselves and with

---

[22] *Mishneh Torah*, Hilchot Deot 2:3.

whatever he finds."[23] The *shefal ruach*, however, in addition to behavior of the type just described, must also be prepared to act in a manner that would express his sense of personal insignificance when relating to the Almighty. Thus Bachya cites, in order to illustrate, the act of Aaron, who even though he was the high priest performed the menial task of collecting the ashes of the burnt offering which the fire had consumed, and then the leaping and dancing of King David, behavior unbecoming to a man of his standing, when he was expressing gratitude to God.[24]

A person who is an *anav* in the moral sense, because he does not believe that his achievements justify the judgment that he is superior, does not wish to exercise authority over others. Thus, Shmaya urged us to "hate lordship."[25] But the *shefal ruach*, who emphasizes his own weakness and the strength of others, is patient with human failings. He accepts the foibles and insults of others. The Talmud recommends that we shall be as humble as Hillel. The essence of the tale that follows the precept and is intended to illustrate the humility of Hillel is that he refused to respond with anger to deliberate provocation.[26] He was patient. The Talmud also praises those "who are put to shame and do not put others to shame, hear themselves reviled and do not retort; do everything out of love and rejoice in their own suffering."[27] The patience of the humble leads to forgiveness.

In sum, the humble person entertains certain beliefs, experiences certain feelings, and performs certain actions. In the characterization of humility in this essay, all three—beliefs, feelings, and actions—have been taken into account.

---

[23] *Chovot Halevavot* 6:6.
[24] Ibid.
[25] Avot 1:11.
[26] Shabbat 31a.
[27] Pesachim 88b.

IV

The feeling of self-importance, which under certain conditions is a manifestation of pride, is not entirely proscribed.
According to one view in a talmudic debate, a minimal quantity of pride is required for a specific group of people. In a passage of the Mishnah, a variety of the sense of self-importance is
declared to be mandatory for all. In a well-known passage of
the Talmud we are told:

> R. Hiyya b. Ashi said in the name of Rab: A disciple of the
> sages should possess an eighth [of pride]. R. Huna and
> the son of R. Joshua said: [This small amount of pride]
> crowns him like the awn of the grain. Raba said: [A disci-
> ple of the sages] who possesses [haughtiness of spirit]
> deserves excommunication, and if he does not possess it
> he deserves excommunication. R. Nachman b. Isaac said:
> He should not possess it or part of it. [28]

Setting aside the question of how this debate fares in the
halachah, the following observations are relevant. First, it is the
talmid chacham who is permitted to display the minimum
amount of pride, even according to the sages cited in the passage who condone it. Second, Rashi views the grounds of justification for such pride as entirely practical. He declares in his
commentary that the talmid chacham must have a little arrogance so that the simple-minded will accept his authority. It
would be appropriate to suggest, under the circumstances, that
it is only the act of pride that is deemed necessary, not the corresponding feeling or belief.

The last point is stressed by Meiri, who discussed at great
length the suggestion that certain individuals must exhibit
pride on practical grounds. In addition to the class of talmidei

---

[28] Sotah 5a.

chachamim, he recognized the importance of pride for the smaller body of people who carry the burden of political authority
on their shoulders. They too, but to an even greater degree than
the *talmid chacham,* must arouse reverence and respect. In support of this contention he cites the advice given by Rabbi Judah
the Prince (himself, as mentioned above, outstanding in humility) to the son who was to be his successor: "conduct your
patriarchate with pride."[29] Meiri explains that this quality was
not to become part of the son's nature; he was merely urged to
act in the manner required by his position.[30]

Another form of proud behavior was urged by the Meiri for
the average person, and also for practical reasons. It is the type
of pride that prompts an individual to dissociate himself from
those in society whose behavior is deficient by moral and religious standards. To verify the legitimacy of this category of
practical pride, he cites the following talmudic passage:

> The fair minded of the people in Jerusalem used to act
> thus: They would not sign a deed without knowing who
> would sign with them; they would not sit in judgment
> unless they knew who was to sit with them; and they
> would not sit at a table without knowing their fellow din-
> ers.[31]

By way of further clarification of the permissible forms of
pride, the following observations are in order. First, these
forms describe exceptions to the requirements of the moral
variety of humility, not the religious variety. They describe circumstances in which one may act with pride in relation to other
people, not in relation to God.

---

[29] Ketubot 103b.
[30] *Chibur Hateshuvah* (Talpiot, Yeshiva University, 1963), pp. 121 ff.
[31] Sanhedrin 23a.

Second, the sanction for these exceptions to humble behavior derives from the necessity to enforce moral and religious values upon society and to preserve such values in one's personal behavior. The *talmid chacham* and the *nasi* are obligated to inspire and enforce obedience to laws that express the values of Torah. The individual must refrain from exposing himself to environmental conditions, such as the company of scoundrels, that would weaken his inclination to moral and religious behavior. Proud actions that are approved are therefore motivated by *commitment* rather than by a *sense of self-importance*.

It follows that proud behavior cannot be countenanced if it is irrelevant to the enforcement or preservation of value. This will perhaps explain Maimonides' endorsement of an extreme instance of humility in which a man of deep piety traveling on a ship responded with joy in a situation in which he experienced great humiliation.[32]

The Mishnah, however, in another well-known passage, declares that the feeling of self-importance is a necessity for everyone. "Therefore, every single person is obliged to say: The world was created for my sake."[33] And Rashi explains this declaration to mean, "I am as important as the entire world. Therefore I will not banish myself from the world even with a single transgression."

It should be noted, in the first place, that this feeling of self-importance is required universally, for all. Further, it is not a minimal quantity of self-importance that is urged but a maximum amount. According to Rashi, every single person shall regard himself as equal in value to the entire natural world. Finally it is not merely the *act* which expresses self-importance that is demanded but the correlative feeling and belief.

---

[32] Maimonides' comments on Avot 4:4.
[33] Sanhedrin 37a.

It is also noteworthy that the words that we translate as "pride" and "arrogance" do not occur at all in the Mishnah's formulation of this precept. The Mishnah, then, does not appear to regard this judgment as at all relevant to the question of pride. On the contrary, the very same circumstance cited by the Mishnah in justification of the demand that everyone experience a sense of self-importance is also described as the basis for a sentiment that belongs among the experiences of humility. The circumstance is that man was created alone. This is taken by the Mishnah to imply many things, among them that "one might not say to his fellow, 'My father was greater than thine' [i.e., we must be humble about our ancestry] and that each person shall believe himself to be of the highest value [an experience that seemingly belongs to the category of pride]."

This merely apparent inconsistency may be easily resolved. Its resolution turns on the fact that humility is a relational conception. The humble individual experiences himself as unimportant in relation to God (the religious conception) and to man (the moral conception). But there is no objection to a feeling of self-importance, even to a maximum degree, by any standard and in relation to any object, so long as it is consistent with the experience of unimportance in relation to God and man. In one relation it is even required.

Consider a standard according to which the animate is assigned greater value than the inanimate, the rational is considered superior to the merely animate, and so on. This criterion would clearly assign to man, a being created in the image of God, a very high rank on the scale of value. An individual cannot, in virtue of the possession of this quality, regard himself as important in relation to God, who is its ultimate source, or to his fellow man, who is endowed with the identical quality. On the contrary, it is possible, even required, for him to deem himself unworthy in these relations because man is nothing in the infinite, and because he should always seek excellence in others while diverting attention to his own weakness.

Nevertheless, by the standard here described, a person is obligated to experience a profound sense of self-importance in
virtue of his location in the scheme of creation. Thus King
David who in addressing God compared himself to a worm
groveling in the dust, judged himself (and others), in comparison to the rest of creation, to be but a little less than angels.[34]

This sense of self-importance is required. Rashi, in his comment in the Mishnah cited above, stated that a man's sense of
self-esteem will help him to avoid sin. We may generalize this
view. Man's behavior will depend, to a large extent, on the
image he projects of himself. It makes a great deal of difference
in terms of human action—if we may use some ancient distinc-
tions—whether man regards himself as a rational animal or as
a two-legged animal without feathers. There is a vast difference
between the individual and social behavior patterns of those
who believe themselves to be the bearers of the *tzelem E-lo-kim*
(the image of God) and those who regard themselves as structured bits of matter, complex though they may be, or as brothers to the apes.

The human being logically and psychologically can, and
morally must, view himself as of unlimited value in one relation, though he believes himself unworthy and insignificant in
relation to the divine source of all being.

V

In rabbinic literature, humility is not counted as merely one
of a number of virtues of equal status. Rather is it judged to be
a central virtue[35]—and for several reasons. First, its centrality is
due to its moral status. Again, we turn to a discussion of arro-

---

[34] Psalms 8:6.
[35] There is a talmudic debate (Avodah Zarah 20b) as to whether
chasidut or *anavah* is the greatest of all virtues. Even if one chooses in
favor of *chasidut*, humility may still be regarded as central. Note, too,

gance to shed light on its correlative, humility. The Talmud declares that on one view, arrogance is the moral equivalent of idolatry or atheism.[36] As the Talmud puts it, the arrogant person is to be viewed "as though" (k'ilu) he enjoyed illicit relations with those who are forbidden to him; "as though" he served the gods of the heathens, "as though" he denied the existence of God. On these conceptions, a true estimate of the character of arrogance compels the conclusion that it belongs in the same category as adultery, incest, idolatry, and atheism. If we take into account the moral standard formulated in the literature of the Talmud, we arrive at the result that arrogance is one of the most serious violations of the precepts of Torah. It belongs in the category of the precepts we are not permitted to violate even when threatened with death.

If humility is as much a virtue as arrogance is a vice, we may infer that by the same moral standard, humility ranks among the virtues that are highest on the scale. This is what Nachmanides intended when he wrote that "humility is the best of all the virtues."[37] Bachya echoed the same sentiment when he wrote, "It follows that all virtues are secondary to humility, which is the head and front of them all."[38]

But, second, humility is judged to be central in the Jewish system of ethics because of its practical consequences. Nachmanides regards the virtue of humility as sufficient for

---

that the distinction drawn in the body of this essay between the two conceptions of humility will not be applied in this section, and the distinction is not explicitly made in the sources that will be quoted (with the exception of the passage from the *Chovot Halevavot*). Further, the talmudic passages to which reference will be made do not speak of the concepts of arrogance and humility but of the arrogant and humble *personalities*. It may be assumed that the typical arrogant or humble personality exemplifies both conceptions.

[36] Sotah 4b ff.

[37] Nachmanides, op. cit.

[38] Bachya, *Chovot Halevavot* 8.

the exemplification of the attitude of reverence, which in turn leads to fear of God and avoidance of sin.

> Through humility there will emerge in your heart the virtue of reverence, for you will consider always from whence you came and where you are going . . . and when you think of all this, you will fear your maker and you will avoid sin.[39]

The Talmud, furthermore, cites the view that arrogance *leads* to adultery. "Anyone who is arrogant will ultimately stumble with another man's wife."[40] The attitude of arrogance is thus declared to be psychologically adequate to the commission of a serious crime. Another major consequence of arrogance is cited in the Torah. "Your heart will be lifted up, and you will forget the Lord your God,"[41] a circumstance which, in turn, may lead to a denial of His existence. All qualities of character involve behavioral consequences, but arrogance leads to results that by the Jewish standard of morality are the most serious of all, namely, atheism and adultery.

These two grounds of the centrality of humility are, however, not independent of each other. A distinction that is relevant to this discussion will serve to clarify their relationship. We must separate virtues (or traits of character) from the actions that illustrate them. A person may be said to possess a certain moral quality if the habit of acting in accordance with the related moral rule has become part of his psychological anatomy. Such a person is expected to exhibit the quality in question, in *most* instances, when the occasion arises. A just man acts justly out of habit, out of an acquired inclination. An action, on the other hand, need not be motivated by a corresponding moral

---

[39] Nachmanides, op. cit.
[40] Sotah 4b.
[41] Deuteronomy 8:14.

habit, that is to say, by a quality of character. It may reflect a passing impulse. An unjust individual does on occasion act justly.

Now a moral theory may include the formulation of a standard by which both actions and habits may be evaluated. Or the moral theory may concern itself exclusively with action. While the primary interest of *halachah* is the specification of rules for action, habits that give rise to behavior in conformity with these rules are endorsed, and those that result in violations of the precepts are rejected. In the case of arrogance, the rejection may take the form of assigning to the habit the identical moral status that belongs to the actions to which it gives rise. This is the view of those who declare that the person with whom arrogance is a habit is to be viewed "as though" he had committed the cardinal crimes of adultery, idolatry, and so on.[42] Or the rejection may take the form of pointing out the consequences of the trait and encouraging its avoidance. Thus, according to another interpretation, arrogance leads to adultery. Analogously, humility may be assigned a moral status identical to that possessed by the actions to which it gives rise; or it may be encouraged on the grounds that it leads to these actions.

In one sense, therefore, humility is central because it results in actions to which Judaism has assigned the highest moral status, and, in one view, because it also belongs to the same moral category. Bachya, however, suggested another ground for its centrality.

---

[42] The talmudic passage in question speaks of *mi she-yesh lo gassie haruach*. Two interpretations of this phrase, as employed here, are in fact possible. (a) It refers to a person who is *actually* experiencing the feeling of arrogance. (b) It refers to a person who has cultivated the *habit* of arrogance, though he may not at the moment be experiencing the relevant sentiments. The severity of the pronouncements, however, lend support to the interpretation that it is the habit rather than an individual act that is the subject of the judgment.

Bachya identifies humility as a necessary condition for the possession of any of the other virtues, that is to say, a person cannot exemplify any other virtue in his behavior if he does not possess humility. "It also follows that no virtue can exist in anyone whose heart is devoid of humility before God."[43] According to Bachya, therefore, not every humble person is penitent, but no one can be penitent if he is not humble.

Bachya's claim, however, is not clear. Two questions are relevant. First, did Bachya insist on "humility before God" as a necessary condition for the exercise of all virtues, including those that are characteristic of human relations, or did he have in mind only those that belong under the heading of piety. But of even greater significance is the second question, which incidentally is not unrelated to the first. When Bachya demands humility as a necessary ingredient of all virtues, is he making a factual claim or proposing a definition? Is he declaring that humility, on the Jewish view, enters into the definition of each virtue, in which case, by definition, no quality of character that is not accompanied by humility could be a virtue. Or are the various virtues sufficiently defined without the inclusion of the element of humility, in which case the statement that humility is a necessary condition of all virtues—that is, that wherever one *finds* virtue, there one *finds humility*—is a factual generalization in regard to human nature.

It would appear, from factual considerations, that Bachya's claim can be defended only if it formulates a generalization about the definition of the virtues in the context of Jewish ethical theory. Consider the illustration that Bachya employed: repentance. Suppose repentance means no more than regret for past transgressions accompanied by a resolution to avoid similar violations in the future. Experience provides illustrations of people who are not endowed with the virtue of humility before

---

[43] Bachya, *Chovot Halevavot* 8.

God (atheists, for example), but who recognize and acknowledge the sanction of certain moral rules, are guilt-stricken when they violate them, experience a sense of regret on those occasions, and affirm the appropriate resolution. If Bachya's claim is correct, however, this sequence would not be a genuine example of repentance, a conclusion that could be maintained only if Judaism were held to define the virtues in such a way that nothing can be a virtue if it does not include the sense of "humility before God."[44]

On this interpretation, it is probable that Bachya regards "humility before God" as an ingredient, not merely of the virtues in the category of piety, but of all virtues. For Bachya is not engaged in the task of making religious definitions. Accordingly, by way of illustration, one may on the basis of purely social considerations extend the hand of generosity to the poor. But it would not be *tzedakah* unless the act is also motivated or, at least, accompanied by "humility before God."

---

[44] This conclusion also seems to be suggested by the passage in Bachya. After making the point that "no moral quality can possibly exist in any one whose heart is devoid of humility before God," he writes, "Thus also the beginning of repentance is loneliness, submissiveness, and humility, as Scripture saith: 'If My people, which are called by My name, shall be humble themselves and pray and seek My face' (II Chronicles 7:14). Further it is said, 'They have humbled themselves; I will not destroy them' (ibid. 12:7)." In this passage, as Bachya apparently interpreted it, divine forgiveness as a response to repentance is described as following on humility. Thus humility is at the core of the act of repentance; it is not something that stands at the periphery of penitence and with which it is merely invariably connected.

Chapter 11

Reverence

A religious theory of ethics should include a discussion of reverence, an attitude that is an essential component of the response to the holy. In view of the fact that all *mitzvot*, including the moral and ethical ones, derive from the Torah, a source that is ultimate in sanctity, the posture of reverence is obligatory in relation to moral principles. In addition, when we fulfill our moral obligations to others, we recognize simultaneously that the moral imperatives also flow from the sanctity of the human being, who bears the image of God, and in the case of the Jew, from the additional sanctity rooted in the Sinaitic Covenant in which he participates. It is therefore not sufficient, in moral conduct, to experience a sense of moral obligation; it is also essential to exhibit the attitude of reverence toward the moral imperatives commanded by Torah and toward the human being in virtue of his sanctity.

The Hebrew word for "reverence" is *yirah*, an ambiguous term that connotes both fear and reverence. How to interpret this word depends on the context in which it occurs and sometimes, when both meanings seem appropriate, on the preference of the commentator.

We are instructed to revere (or fear) our parents, to revere (or fear) our teachers, to revere (or fear) God. Fear and reverence connote two different attitudes. Fear is a state of anxiety associated with the anticipated experience of pain. Reverence, on the other hand, is felt when we are aware of or in the presence of that which is of transcendent value. Reverence, it should be noted, is also more than respect. The latter is an appreciation of that which is essentially human, for example, achievement in the realm of nature. We *respect* those who have accomplished much, especially when we recognize that we as individuals and the society to which we belong have profited from their contributions. But we *revere* those who embody *values* which are objective and of surpassing worth, and which we treasure independently of the fact that we may be beneficiaries. Both attitudes—fear and reverence—may be appropriate, in different circumstances, in relation to parents, teachers of sacred texts, and the Supreme Being. We are afraid of punishment, but we are filled with awe, painless though it may be, in the presence of one who is or represents the holy. The feeling of awe is essentially appropriate when the one—whether individual or object—who inspires it is perceived as ultimate in value.

The Talmud inquires as to the meaning of the term *yirah* as applied to the relation of a child to a parent, and responds with some examples:

He shall not stand in his [the parent's] place, he shall not sit on his seat, he shall not contradict him, nor shall he intervene [when his parent is involved in a controversy with an adversary] to declare that his parent is correct.[1]

Such conduct is clearly not a manifestation of fear; it is also more than respect. If a child refuses to occupy his father's seat at the head of the table, even in his father's absence, it is not because of the anticipation of punishment should he be caught

---

[1] Kidushin 31b.

in the act, nor is it merely a sign of respect, which normally does not require the maintenance of such distance from objects occupied by a parent; it is, rather, a demonstration of reverence.

Indeed, there are two obligations in the relation of a child toward parents. In addition to *yirah*, the obligation to revere, there is also *kavod*, the obligation to honor or respect, which according to the Talmud is exhibited in the following ways: "He must give him [his parent] food and drink, he must clothe and cover him, and take him in and out."[2] Respect and reverence are not mutually exclusive. Obviously, where reverence is an obligation, respect is also appropriate.

The obligation a student has toward his *rebbe* (his teacher of sacred texts) is also described in terms of *kavod* and *yirah*. Maimonides declares:

> Just as a man is commanded to honor and revere his father, so is he commanded to honor and revere his *rebbe*, and even more than his father. For his father brings him into this world, while his *rebbe*, from whom he learns wisdom, brings him into the world to come.[3]

In relation to a *rebbe*, however, the word *yirah* may have the dual meaning of both fear and reverence. It is, for example, a requirement of the Passover Seder that a Jew lean on his left side during certain stages of the meal as a mark of freedom. The Talmud declares that this requirement does not apply to a student who is present at his *rebbe*'s table on the night of Passover, because of the principle that *morah rabcha kemorah shamayim*, "the reverence [or fear] of your *rebbe* should be like the reverence [or fear] of Heaven."[4]

---

[2] Ibid.
[3] *Mishneh Torah*, Hilchot Talmud Torah 5:1.
[4] Pesachim 108a.

The preferred interpretation is that this principle refers to the attitude of reverence. Rabbi Yitzchak Ze'ev Soloveitchik, however, explained that the suspension of this obligation is rooted in the fact that the fear of one's *rebbe* renders the feeling of freedom unattainable and cannot be exhibited through any gesture, for example, leaning,[5] so there is no point to performing it. It appears, therefore, that in this context he assigns the meaning of fear to the concept of *yirah*.

The obligation to display *yirah* in relation to God is clearly to be expressed in the form of both fear and reverence. There is the fear of the consequences of transgression (*yirat ha-onesh*) and reverence for the Infinite and Transcendent Being who is of Supreme Value (*yirat ha-hitromemut*). The Torah associates painful experiences in the life of the people of Israel with violations of principles of Torah. Two passages, referred to as the *tochachah*, which depict the tragic conditions that a rebellious people must endure as a consequence of sin, have the effect of generating fear. The need for reverence, on the other hand, is implicit in the declaration of the patriarch Abraham, who, appealing to God on behalf of the people of Sodom, introduced his petition with the declaration that he was, in relation to the Supreme Being, but "dust and ashes." Such humility, which expresses an appreciation for the transcendent and infinite value of the Supreme Being, is the highest expression of reverence.

Our purpose will be to identify the elements of reverence and to indicate its significance in the life of both the individual and society.

Reverence is manifested in the maintenance of distance. In his *The Idea of the Holy*, Rudolf Otto explains that the holy is to be understood in terms of two components: one, that the holy is overpowering and unapproachable; the other, that the holy

---

5 *Haggadah shel Pesach* (Jerusalem: Oraisa, 1983), p. 94.

is precious beyond all human conception. God, of course, is supremely holy. The holy, accordingly, is *dreaded* because it overwhelms; but it also fascinates and *attracts* because of its infinite value. This combination of repulsion and attraction constitutes the experience of distance. The finite human being finds the Supreme Being irresistible, but at the same time, because of his limitations, unapproachable. He wants, simultaneously, to move closer and to withdraw. He is prompted to maintain distance.

The human being's desire to approach ever more closely is illustrated in the exposition of Rabbi Naftali Tzvi Yehudah Berlin (also known as the Netziv) of the biblical passage describing the episode that led to the death of Nadav and Abihu, the two sons of Aaron. The Torah relates that "They brought upon the altar a strange fire which they were not commanded to do." The Netziv writes:

> They entered the sanctuary with a burning passion of the love of God, but the Torah declares that, while the love of God is precious to God, it is not to be displayed in a manner that He did not command.[6]

One ought not to get too close. Notwithstanding the urge to become more deeply involved with the Supreme Being, and this is the normal impulse of the religious personality, he is instructed to withdraw and maintain distance.

When the Almighty descended upon Mount Sinai and communicated the ten declarations to the people of Israel, He warned in advance, "You shall erect a boundary for the people," that is, establish a barrier between the people and the mountain which they are not to penetrate. The mountain, so long as the Almighty's Presence was upon it, was holy, and dis-

---

[6] Commentary on Leviticus 10:1.

tance had to be maintained. Distance is also an imperative in the sanctuary. Those who are not priests are prohibited from entering certain parts of the sanctuary, and the Holy of Holies may not be invaded even by the high priest except on the Day of Atonement.

The maintenance of distance is, on the one hand, an *obligation*. On the other hand, distance is a normal *psychological response* in the presence of the holy. When the people heard the words of God at Sinai, they were terrified and said to Moses, "You speak to us and we shall hear; let God not speak to us lest we die."[7]

The requirement of distance is also implicit in the rabbinic equation identifying sanctity with separation. The prophet Isaiah declared, "Holy, holy, holy is the Lord of Hosts." Malbim explains the threefold use of the word "holy" as meaning that He is separated in three ways. He is separated from all forms; He is separated from all matter; He is separated from all privation.[8] These varieties of separation create chasms that no human being can bridge. The inevitable result is distance.

The obligation to maintain distance in relation to a sacred object implies that the holy shall be left intact without modification. If it is holy, it ought not to be manipulated. Human beings, however, often seek to transform the sacred to accommodate it to human preferences and inclination. The obligation to maintain distance implies that man ought to refrain from acting upon such inclinations.

There is a tendency in the Jewish community to transform the Torah, to excise many of its commandments or at least to judge them inapplicable, in the interests of being relevant. Contemporary human experience has been so enticing, often even intoxicating, that many have felt it necessary to adjust the

---

7 Exodus 20:16.
8 Commentary on Isaiah 6:3.

Torah to make it conform to modern tastes and criteria. The result has been the repudiation of large segments of the sacred text. It is a process that demonstrates, wherever it occurs, that the sense of reverence and the appreciation of the sanctity of Torah has been lost.

It is the sanctity of the synagogue that primarily, according to Rabbi Joseph B. Soloveitchik, militates against any change to its structure. Some argue that men and women should not be allowed to sit together during prayer because such contiguity renders concentration in prayer impossible. This, according to Rabbi Soloveitchik, is not the fundamental reason for separating them. Maimonides states that the biblical imperative applicable to the Holy Temple, "You shall revere My sanctuary," prohibits any modification in its structure. Rabbi Soloveitchik maintains that this biblical precept, according to Maimonides, is equally applicable to the synagogue.[9]

Reverence and distance are also mandatory in interpersonal relations. To the extent that we recognize sanctity in the person, we have a duty to exhibit reverence and maintain distance. That distance should be interpreted in terms of the obligations spelled out in the sacred texts. "Thou shalt not steal," "Thou shalt not kill" assert commands which are essential not only because society cannot survive unless they are obeyed, but more significantly, because they are expressions of the sanctity of the human being.

Especially is there a need to exhibit reverence and maintain distance in the area of medical practice. A physician, allowed by society to take risks with the lives of his patients, should perceive them as endowed with a level of sanctity that instills reverence when he undertakes a procedure that may abbreviate their life span, diminish its quality, or result in their death.

---

[9] Moshe Meiselman, "The Rav, Feminism and Social Policy: An Insider's View," Tradition 33, p.15.

The need for this perception is underscored in a talmudic passage:

> He who enters to visit the sick shall not sit on a couch or a chair but shall cover his head [as with a *talit*—Rashi explains so that he will focus only on the patient and not allow himself to be distracted] and sit before him [presumably in a less comfortable posture] because God is present at the head of the person who is sick.[10]

The physician's constant awareness of the Divine Presence during his medical ministrations will induce an attitude of reverence and impose distance from any practice that would represent a violation of God's word or the sanctity of the person who is his patient.

II

Another characteristic of reverence, to which reference has already been made but which needs elaboration, is that it is invariably manifested as a response to the transcendent. Fear is prompted by self-interest; it is an experience in circumstances that threaten one's well-being. Reverence is a sense of awe in the presence of that which is of infinite value and in relation to which considerations of personal advantage, though they may exist, are recognized as of little consequence.

A rabbinic luminary noted that the word *vayirah* and its grammatical variation, *nora*, which occur in two biblical contexts and describe the responses of Jacob in two different episodes, have the meaning of fear in one and reverence in the other. When Jacob was preparing to encounter Esau after a two-decade separation, convinced that his brother had not forgiven him for appropriating his blessing, we are told that Jacob

---

[10] Shabbat 12b.

was afraid (*vayirah*). He was concerned about the harm he and his family might suffer. It was an anxiety prompted by self-interest. When, on the other hand, he lay down at night and dreamed of angels ascending and descending a ladder with God at its top, upon waking, he exclaimed, "How awesome (*nora*) is this place; this is none other than the dwelling of God, and this is the gate of heaven." Here the response was not fear but reverence, the sense that he had encountered a Being of Infinite Value.[11]

In truth, both of these attitudes occur in Jacob's response to Esau. In anticipation of the meeting, the Torah relates that "Jacob was very much afraid and he was distressed." Rashi explains that "he was afraid because he might lose his life, and he was distressed because he might take the lives of others."[12] Obviously, his anxiety about the possible loss of his own life reflects his fear that the outcome of his struggle would be disastrous for him. His concern that he might take the lives of others expresses not fear but reverence for human life because of its inordinate and transcendent value.

Which is the more powerful emotion—fear or reverence? We may suppose that, on the average, reverence is eclipsed by fear. Most people are more inclined to surrender their values than their impulse to self-preservation. Within the Jewish community, the reverse is frequently the case. Jews are often more concerned about avoiding the shedding of blood than securing their own lives.

This is the nature of Jewish heroism. The classical hero of Western civilization rides to glory on the battlefield. He forgoes one variety of self-interest, the preservation of his own life, in the interest of achieving another variety, glory. In the Jewish community, on the other hand, the hero is the one who subor-

---

[11]Rabbi Yaakov Zvi Mecklenburg, *Haktav vehaKabbalah*, Genesis 28:17.

[12] Ibid. 22:7.

dinates and suppresses his fears in order to respond with reverence to transcendent values.

The awareness of transcendent value in persons and moral precepts is a defining feature of Jewish morality. Moral precepts, Judaism teaches, should not be deduced from personal or social considerations. The moral imperative is not dependent on the voice of individual conscience or the need to preserve community; it is, rather, based on an awareness of the infinite value of human life and the transcendent importance of divine imperatives.

III

Another characteristic of reverence is that it inspires. There are varieties of inspiration that generally arise in connection with the ideals mankind has adopted. These ideals are the true, the good, the beautiful, and, above all, the holy. Many are inspired by an elegant resolution of a difficult mathematical puzzle or a novel demonstration of a theorem, by the discovery of a scientific law that yields new insight into nature, by an act of extraordinary courage to enhance the well-being of mankind, by a work of art or literature that embodies the parameters of beauty to an unusual degree, and by the experience of an object such as the Western Wall in Jerusalem whose sanctity is all but palpable. While the other ideals, when they inspire, elicit praise and appreciation, it is only the holy that imbues us with reverence and instills the sense that we are encountering an experience that involves the very purpose of life and the *raison d'être* of human existence.

These ideals confer the highest level of significance upon human life and enable those who embrace them to experience an extraordinary sense of self-worth. In addition, when those who are committed initiate action in behalf of these ideals, they frequently perform extraordinary feats of selflessness. They literally lose themselves in the activity intended to advance the ideals and bring them closer to realization.

Clearly, inspiration is superior to fear as a source of motivation both in the life of the individual and in that of society. In the first place, it affords a sense of well-being which is lacking when actions are prompted by fear alone. But more to the point, fear very often paralyzes; inspiration energizes and motivates. Fear, if it does not paralyze, may prompt action, but it is frequently that of retreating, hiding, or escaping; it does not normally result in acts of creativity. Inspiration, on the other hand, translates in the scientific domain into research productive of new insights into the structure of the universe through the formulation of new scientific laws, and in the aesthetic realm, into achievements in literature, art, music, sculpture, and so on. Or, and this is more to the purpose at hand, it may manifest itself in dedicated action and take the form of unselfish service for a cause supported by an ideal.

In truth, unselfishness can result from a variety of motives. An act of charity may be prompted by *emotional* considerations. The donor experiences sympathy for the deprived or afflicted recipient. It is not difficult to identify with an individual who has suffered tragedy and to imagine oneself in an identical situation of pain and horror, an experience likely to elicit a compassionate response. The unselfish gesture may be *rational*; it may appear as a consequence of an obligation and manifest itself as an expression of duty. It, however, may also result from *inspiration*, from a personal and existential commitment to an ideal that one perceives of surpassing value, and may exhibit itself in the form of self-sacrifice. When inspiration is prompted by the posture of reverence, sacrifice may reach the highest level, namely, the surrender of life.

There have been many martyrs in the history of the Jewish people who gave their lives for the sake of God and Torah. While the same degree of self-sacrifice is not normally required in circumstances that are essentially moral,[13] such a context also allows for the religious response of reverence and its attendant self-sacrifice. The result may not be the surrender of life, but it will be a higher level of sacrifice than what is appropriate and normally manifested in the pursuit of aesthetic and scientific ideals and even of the moral ideal when not informed by the holy.

The relation between fear and reverence is itself significant. The two are inversely proportional to each other; that is, the greater the reverence, the less the fear. Reverence for God and His Torah prompted the great Jewish martyrs of the past— Rabbi Akiva is the best-known—to submit to death when their lives were threatened for the alleged crime of teaching and observing the precepts of Torah. They may have experienced fear, but it was diminished, perhaps even eclipsed. Rabbi Akiva expressed joy in the face of the opportunity to exhibit love for God in the act of supreme sacrifice.

IV

Reverence also contributes to solidarity in human relations and social life. Solidarity is a form of association that reflects, first of all, the fact that the members of a community understand their relationship to be based on commitment to the ideals that define the community rather than on coercion and the fear that is its concomitant. Indeed, this is one of the differences between unity and solidarity. Unity can be achieved by threats; the specter of anti-Semitism unites Jews of different ideological commitments in the interests of self-defense.

---

[13] The obvious exception is in the case where an individual is threatened with death if he does not take the life of another. He is instructed by halachic precept to surrender his life, and if moved by religious commitments, he will do so because of a sense of reverence.

Solidarity is rooted in commitment. But further, solidarity also arises as a result of the reverence that members of a community mutually experience in relation to each other because of the recognition on the part of each of the image of God possessed by the other. Judaism seeks to instill in its adherents not merely a sense of unity but one of solidarity by requiring reverence toward that which is sacred in the ultimate, namely, human beings and the values embodied in Torah precepts.

Solidarity translates into strength. The person whose behavior is controlled by fear is motivated by self-interest. When he confronts a life-threatening situation or even the possibility of discomfort in the service of his community, and he could avoid it without exposing himself to punitive consequences, he will in all likelihood do so. A person who is committed—especially when the object of his commitment is a community that he perceives as holy—will be inspired to perform actions that are selfless. In the process, his feelings of association and involvement and his identification with others in his community of commitment will be deepened and strengthened.

It is generally recognized that fear is an indispensable means of exercising community control and, in the best of political circumstances, to ensure the reign of justice and peace. This is an inevitable consequence of human nature, which is not readily malleable and easily molded into an ideal shape. Indeed, the existence of a government is understood by the rabbis as instilling fear in the hearts of the people. "Pray for the peace of the kingdom, because were it not for fear, each man would swallow the other alive."[14] The Torah, even in a theocracy, requires the appointment of a judiciary and a police force to ensure the implementation of justice and the maintenance of standards. "You shall appoint judges and officers in all your gates." Nevertheless there is substantial disagreement as to whether

---

[14] Avot 3:2.

the element of fear should be controlling in society, or whether the goal should be to inspire citizens of the Jewish state to respond with reverence.

There is a dispute in the rabbinic literature as to whether the creation of a political state, which normally utilizes coercion to assure social harmony, is biblically mandatory or merely permitted. The Torah declares, "Place a king over you." Maimonides asserts that it is obligatory to do so.

Three commandments were assigned to the people of Israel when they entered the Holy Land: to designate a king, as it is written, "Place a king over yourself"; to eradicate the memory of the Amalekites, as it is written, "Eradicate the memory of the Amalekites"; and to build the holy Temple, as it is written, "You shall seek the place where His Spirit dwells, and you shall come there."[15]

It follows from the juxtaposition in Maimonides' listing of the three commandments that the designation of a sovereign, that is, the creation of a political state, is in the same category of obligation as the eradication of the Amalekites and the building of the Temple, that is to say, it is mandatory. According to Abrabanel, however, it is merely allowed.[16] It is, on his view, preferable to avoid introducing a temporal power into the life of the nation. The reason is that social harmony and tranquility should result from responding to the Almighty's commands with reverence rather than from fear of the punishment imposed by a sovereign. If, however, the people of Israel desire it to ensure their security, Abrabanel teaches, it is permitted. Nevertheless, the ideal state is one that is shaped and guided by principles that inspire reverence.

---

[15] *Mishneh Torah*, Hilchot Melachim 1:1.
[16] In his commentary on Deuteronomy 17:14.

Chapter 12

Religion and Morality

A much-debated issue in moral philosophy is the relation between morality and religion. Religion, in general, comprises two components: (1) transcendental beliefs, such as God created the world, He communicated with man, He offers redemption and salvation to mankind; and (2) a set of obligations, such as engage in prayer, honor parents, refrain from theft, murder, envy, and so on. It is a characteristic of Judaism as a religion that it assigns priority to the second of these features. The *mitzvah*, or commandment, is more important than transcendental beliefs. Further, the Torah's commandments are twofold. Some focus on man's direct involvement with the Divine Being and require the performance of such precepts as fasting on *Yom Kippur*, eating in a *sukkah* on the festival of Sukkot, and refraining from various forms of work on the Sabbath. Others are directed to interpersonal obligations and consequently are moral. The latter will be the focus of our concern.

Moral discussions generally address one or all of three major questions: (1) What is the content of the moral system, that is, which precepts are declared to be moral? (2) What is the sanction for these precepts, that is, what makes them right? (3) What is the source of motivation for them, that is, what prompts human beings to obey them? The relation of morality

178

to religion will be explored in all three of these respects. There is one additional question that will be addressed, namely, what are the implications of religious belief for moral conduct? Many are of the opinion that a religious person is inevitably, even necessarily, a moral person. Is this, in fact, the case?

I

First, the content! Moral rules are generally associated with an ideal. There are three ideals that are the subject of moral discussion and the basis for human conduct. One of these is happiness, the second is justice, and the third is mercy. Rules derived from the ideal of happiness are here designated as ethical rather than moral. The term "ethics" is reserved in our discussion for a system of precepts that delineates conduct intended to bring happiness to an individual. The thrust of this ideal, as understood at least in ancient days, is not essentially the obligations human beings have toward each other, but the rules whose application is indispensable to the achievement of happiness and thus not essentially moral.[1]

Notwithstanding, moral philosophers have tried to demonstrate an invariable causal connection between moral precepts and human happiness. On their view, a theory of ethics will also include precepts that describe acceptable conduct toward

---

[1] Ethical and moral rules need not be distinguished in a mutually exclusive manner. In some theories, as noted here, the observance of moral rules is perceived as a means to the achievement of happiness. Notwithstanding, there are theories that separate these two sets of rules sharply, claiming that if the goal is personal happiness, the rule derived from it cannot be moral (Kant). Further, even theories that focus exclusively on happiness and adopt moral principles because they are means to its achievement grant that moral rules are observed as a matter of habit because they are perceived as right (Mill). In any case, it would be appropriate to label rules that guide interpersonal relations as "ethical" rather than "moral" when they are intended to achieve happiness.

others. They are introduced, not because of the perception that they impose obligations independent of self-interest, but to ensure the happiness of those who are guided by them. This analysis applies as well to modern utilitarian thinkers. Many of them regard pleasure as the *summum bonum,* the ultimate good, and they identify pleasure with happiness. The rules they formulate are, in the last analysis, guidelines to be followed by those who seek happiness. Included among the rules are precepts that guide human relations. But once again, there is a difference between the suggestion that certain rules of an interpersonal character are advantageous to practitioners engaged in the pursuit of happiness, and the assertion that these rules are obligatory because of extrapersonal considerations.

Further, moral rules also divide into two categories. The ideals of justice and of mercy both imply precepts of conduct, but of different sorts. The former requires such traits as honesty, integrity, and fairness, and the latter, thoughtfulness, sensitivity, compassion, and love. Judaism recognizes the difference between them and, as already noted, assigns priority to the latter.

The assertion that the precepts of justice and mercy belong to two different categories can be inferred from the rabbinic judgments, discussed earlier, that they derive from different ancient sources. Precepts of justice, they taught, are articulated in the seven Noachide precepts enunciated at the time of the Flood, which are incumbent on all mankind, while the obligations to engage others in relations manifesting loving-kindness were accepted by the Israelites enslaved in Egypt through the instrumentality of a covenant. This difference between the rules of justice and mercy is obvious. The rules of justice were imposed on mankind; those of mercy were voluntarily accepted by the Israelites by covenant.

There is a modern theory of natural law to the effect that certain moral rules are indispensable to the preservation of human society and that such laws arise in response to human inter-

ests.[2] A community cannot survive if its members do not
adhere to rules that prohibit, for example, fraud, theft, and
murder. But it has been maintained, contrary to Jewish doctrine, that a viable society need not depend on the rules that
flow from the ideal of mercy. A society built on rugged individualism, for instance, is capable of surviving. Some theories
of ethics, essentially egoistical, advocate precisely that kind of
social arrangement. Judaism's introduction of the precepts of
mercy into the domain of obligatory morality, and its insistence
on their priority, directs attention to the Jewish view that the
survival of mankind depends on the widespread implementation of mercy in human affairs.

II

The second question that needs to be addressed pertains to
the *justification* of moral rules. What is it that makes them right?
Some Jewish theologians endorse the view, previously discussed, that moral principles can be derived *rationally* even
without the benefit of a commanding Supreme Being. If this is
the case, then the claim that the principles were also divinely
ordained needs to be interpreted as providing an additional
source of justification for them. If reason is not a satisfactory
basis for the derivation of moral precepts, the divine command
is to be perceived as the foundation of their sanction and
authority.

On the assumption that morality does indeed have a rational
foundation, it is legitimate to ask whether only precepts of justice are to be construed as rational or whether rationality is also
the basis of precepts deduced from the ideal of mercy. We have
already examined different interpretations of the claim that
moral rules are rationally grounded. On the view that an exam-

---

[2] Cf. Morris R. Cohen, *Reason and Nature* (Glencoe, Ill.: Free Press,
1931), pp. 401–25.

ination of the nature of the universe will yield both physical
and moral laws, it is not evident that precepts of mercy are
rationally mandated. Another view has it that moral laws are
instilled into the human mind at birth. A modern variation of
this doctrine is that of Immanuel Kant, who claimed that the
conscience, the voice of practical reason, commands conduct
that can be deduced from a rational principle which he labeled
the "categorical imperative." On the Kantian view, it can be
shown—at least he thought so[3]—that the principles of mercy
are also rationally grounded, that is, that they too are deducible
from the categorical imperative. Still another basis for rationality is the utilitarian consideration to the effect that unless people live by moral rules, certain social aims—for example, the
survival of society—would not be achieved. One who believes
that society can survive on a foundation of justice alone could
argue that while the principles deduced from the ideal of justice are rational, those derived from the ideal of mercy are not.
If people refrain from theft and murder and mutually respect
each other's rights, society might flourish even if every one of
its citizens displayed a posture of resistance to generosity and
compassion that made him totally indifferent to the fate of his
neighbors. There have been periods in human history when
such an attitude prevailed.

But there is another question that must be addressed in this
connection. The assertion that reason prescribes moral rules
and the claim that man has an obligation to abide by them are
not identical. Granted that the precepts enunciated by reason
are rational, does it follow that the conclusion that man is obligated to accept them is equally rational? It would be if the two
propositions were *logically* related. But are they? It has been
demonstrated that we cannot, according to the canons of logic,
deduce an "ought" from an "is," that is, an obligation from a

---

[3] The obligation to help the poor is one of the cases Kant explicitly
cites as coming under the categorical imperative.

fact. One may agree that it is indeed a fact that reason issues moral imperatives, or that social circumstances require them, but the question remains, does this imply that man is obligated?

Clearly, the justification of man's obligation does not rest on logical inference. Consider, by way of example, an argument that is theologically based and concludes that there is an obligation to avoid theft. The premises are the following: (1) God exists; (2) God communicated the Torah, which consists of commandments; (3) one of these is "Thou shalt not steal." The conclusion is: man is obligated not to steal. It is obvious that the conclusion does not follow logically from the premises. This invalid argument can be turned into one that is valid by introducing a fourth premise (the theological postulate of obligation), which states: (4) when God commands, men are obligated to obey. It then does follow logically that man has an obligation not to steal. The essential point is that unless proposition (4) is included among the premises, the conclusion that man has an obligation to avoid theft is not logically compelling. The same point can be made if the source of obligation is regarded as rational. Unless there is included among the premises the assertion "man is obligated to obey the dictates of reason" (the rational postulate of obligation), in addition to the proposition "reason declares that stealing is wrong," the conclusion that man has a duty to refrain from stealing is not logically sound.

In short, if we are to speak of moral obligation as rational, the meaning must be that the *obligation* itself, in some sense, arises out of the rational faculty (i.e., it is a postulate of reason). It does not mean that man's obligation to abide by moral rules is logically deduced from the fact that reason *prescribes* them. Hence, moral theories differ on the basis of the axiom of obligation that each postulates. Some base obligation on the Divine Will, others on a mandate of reason, some on a social imperative, and still others on some other foundation, perhaps of an intuitive sort.

The question that needs to be addressed is whether the religious postulate of obligation has implications for a moral life that differ significantly from the corresponding postulates based on rational, social, or intuitive grounds.

III

One difference is obvious; it relates to the degree of motivation. Every moral theory, in addition to enunciating a postulate of obligation, must also provide a psychological theory of motivation. Given that the moral theory is authoritative and imposes obligation, what motivates an individual to abide by it?

There are different sources of motivation. One is self-interest. Many have argued, rightly or wrongly, that obedience to moral rules is advantageous to those who act in consonance with them. To violate the rules is to risk suffering a way of life that is inherently unsatisfactory, that is, to experience humiliation if the transgression is discovered, to be ostracized if the community is sufficiently enraged, and even to receive punishment of a serious sort if the violation turns out to be not merely immoral but criminal. Ancient Greek and Roman thinkers and modern utilitarians who relate moral conduct to the ideal of happiness have generally adopted this doctrine; they argue that the inevitable consequence of violating moral rules is that the transgressor cannot achieve happiness, the goal for which every human being strives. Accordingly, to adhere to moral imperatives is to assure oneself, at least in some measure, of leading a satisfactory life.

The self-interested variety of motivation is also incorporated into a religious scheme of things. The religious concept of *yirah* expresses the manner in which a Jew shall relate to the Supreme Being. It is sometimes translated as "reverence" and other times as "fear." *Yirat shamayim* is either reverence toward heaven or fear of heaven, and if the latter, it means that an individual is prompted to obey out of fear of divine retribution. This too is motivation prompted by self-interest.

Another motive for obedience is habit, which carries with it a power of its own. Habit cultivated by education and training, as a result of which we may frequently act contrary to our own advantage, is arguably more compelling than self-interest. John Stuart Mill maintained that as a result of cultivated habit, society can instill within each individual a feeling of unity with his compatriots, a sense that his well-being is so dependent on the well-being of the whole that he will not be able to imagine doing harm to society without experiencing a powerful feeling that he is doing injury to himself. Mill wrote:

> If we now suppose this feeling of unity to be taught as a religion and the whole force of education, of institutions, and of opinion directed, as it once was in the case of religion, to make every person grow up from infancy surrounded on all sides both by the profession and practice of it, I think that no one who can realize this conception will feel any misgivings about the sufficiency of the ultimate sanction for the happiness morality. . . . The deeply rooted conception which every individual even now has of himself as a social being tends to make him feel it one of his natural wants that there should be harmony between his feelings and aims and those of his fellow creatures.[4]

As this thinker saw it, education, aided by the force of habit, inculcates in the minds and hearts of a community's members the sense that their interests as individuals and that of the community as a whole are identical. In other words, what is good for the community is good for each individual. Since obedience

---

[4] Mill, *Utilitarianism* (New York: Liberal Arts Press; 1953), pp. 35–36.

to moral precepts on the part of citizens is in the community's best interest, it follows from this reasoning that it will also be perceived by those appropriately trained and habituated as advantageous to the individual. But since this perception is induced by habit, it constitutes a source of motivation that does not depend on self-interest.

Another source of motivation is the satisfaction of knowing that moral behavior is a response to the demands of reason. There is a sense of well-being attached to the notion that one is conducting his life according to a higher standard. The moral standard, on this interpretation, is not adopted by an individual because of self-interest, nor is it instilled as a habit by a community to further the community's interest; it rather involves the recognition that reason, the function of man that distinguishes him from the animal kingdom, requires obedience to that standard. Reason, on this interpretation, is seen as elevating, and its imperatives as ennobling. Its demands, independent of self-interest, are believed to express what is best and inspiring in the very nature of man.

But none of these sources of motivation can match that supplied by religion, and particularly by Judaism. To begin with, the principal source of moral rules is a Supreme Being who possesses infinite authority. One cannot be aware of that authority without being overwhelmed by its infinite power. The sense of guilt experienced by a moral individual who is indifferent to religion when he transgresses is based on his awareness that what he did was wrong, that he has violated a moral rule. The guilt experienced by a religious individual when he transgresses is based principally on the fact that he has disobeyed God. There is a commentary in the Talmud to the effect that while the Torah distinguishes among different categories of sin and assigns them punishments of different degrees of severity, in principle any infraction of a biblical rule constitutes an affront against God and deserves the supreme penalty.[5] Thus, even while the religious person may recognize the inherent merit of the moral precepts biblically prescribed because of the considerations adumbrated above, he is even more sensitive, and therefore responsive, to the fact that they are expressions of the will of God.

But Judaism introduces an additional dimension into this discussion. Even as it recognizes that there is a divinely imposed obligation addressed to the entire human race, it also insists on a particularistic obligation, embraced by the Jewish community through the instrumentality of a covenant. The Talmud explains, as already noted above, that all mankind is obligated to obey the seven Noachide commandments. These obligations are not dependent on a communal gesture of acceptance. It is clear from the talmudic interpretation of the source of the Noachide commandments that they are regarded as imposed. According to Nachmanides, these commandments are, in fact, generic *principles* that subsume an expanded set of moral precepts. He writes:

> He [God] commanded them with regard to the laws of theft, deception, oppression, paying an employee in a timely way, the laws of the bailee, rape, seduction, damages, the laws of the lender and the borrower, and the laws of economic transactions, and so on, similar to the laws commanded to Jews.[6]

---

[5] Rashi writes on the phrase *malkot bimkom mita omedet* (Sanhedrin 10a), "Because he transgressed against his creator's injunction, he is deserving of death."

[6] Commentary on Genesis 35:13. Nachmanides takes issue with Maimonides, who offered another interpretation of the Noachide laws.

These laws, principles of justice, clearly embody and express the moral ideals of Judaism which Judaism holds to be incumbent on all men.

But, in addition, the religion of Judaism is based on a covenantal agreement by which the people of Israel undertook to observe the entire Torah—which also includes the Noachide commandments. The implication is that in the Jewish perspective, there are two bases of a theological nature for the sanction of moral precepts—one, universal and imposed, and the second, particularistic and voluntary. The latter results from the fact that the people of Israel at Sinai committed themselves by covenant to live by all the precepts contained in the Torah. The people of Israel accordingly have a dual relation with God: He is a Sovereign who legislates for all His creatures, including the people of Israel, and the Covenantal Partner in relation to whom the people of Israel assumed obligations.

IV

And yet, it is clear from experience that the motivation for the observance of biblical precepts is much stronger in the case of those that are essentially ritualistic and delineate norms of conduct in relation to God, than of those that are moral and focus on human interpersonal relations. This is a comprehensible state of affairs which follows from two considerations.

First, it has something to do with the way the concept of man's relationship to man is understood. It is usually held, not only that a man has obligations toward others, but also that the *others* are the *source* of these obligations. It is held that it is the sacred nature of man, perceived as a bearer of the divine image, which imposes moral obligations within the human community. On the other hand, one could argue that it is not man but God who is the Source of all moral obligations, and that in responding morally to human beings we are, in effect, fulfilling obligations, not to man, but to God. This is, in fact, the way most interpreters of Judaism understand moral obligation. But the popular perception is otherwise, for it holds that it is man who generates such obligations, a focus that eclipses the fact that God is the Supreme Moral Legislator. Given the popular understanding, it is not difficult to take the next step and conclude that fulfilling obligations to the infinite and omnipotent God is considerably more important than responding morally to finite man.

The popular perception is supported by another consideration. In Jewish practice, a blessing is recited as an introduction to the performance of a *mitzvah*. The formula of the blessing includes the phrase "Who sanctified us with His commandments and commanded us." The articulation of this phrase obviously enhances the awareness that one is responding to God's will. The problem is that this blessing is not recited in anticipation of the performance of all commandments. Maimonides explains that it applies only to those that instruct the Jew how to relate to God.[7] In effect, this means that a blessing is never recited in anticipation of the fulfillment of a moral imperative. The Jew's consciousness of an involvement with God when he responds morally to other human beings is accordingly weakened.[8]

V

The motivation to comply with moral imperatives is indeed stronger when such obedience is required by religion. Is this, however, always the case? Does religion always advocate con-

---

[7] *Mishneh Torah*, Hilchot Berachot 11:2.
[8] This explanation of the reason for the weaker motivation prompted by moral as opposed to purely religious commandments has been attributed to Rabbi Joseph B. Soloveitchik.

duct that satisfies the dictates of morality? It is well known that many crimes have been committed in the name of religion. How does religion respond to allegations that in some of its forms, it often promotes criminal behavior? In truth, different religions can be classified by the diverse ways they relate religious obligations to moral imperatives.

On one interpretation, moral principles are simply suspended when they conflict with religious imperatives. Such a view was expressed by a religious thinker who interpreted the biblical episode of the binding of Isaac as an instance of the "teleological suspension of the ethical,"[9] which means that religion is assigned priority and superiority to a point where it eclipses moral mandates. The demands of faith, at least to the religious mind, could appear to have greater authority than the universal precepts applicable to a finite moral community. Advocates of this view unabashedly declare that moral precepts have no claim on the conduct of those who are genuinely religious when the claim conflicts with the demands of faith.

Another approach, one that is more popular, is that of redefinition. On this view, religion is not indifferent to human welfare, which, among other things, depends on the application of moral precepts in interpersonal relations. Its advocates passionately declare that they would not deviate from moral commands under any conditions. When however, as sometimes is the case, they take the lives of those (defined as infidels) who reject what they perceive to be religion's fundamental principles, and they often do so indiscriminately, they argue that what they did is not an act of murder. They turn morality on its head and maintain, on the contrary, that such actions are eminently moral on the grounds that the victim is better off dead than afflicted by erroneous theological doctrine. The killing of

---

[9] See the chapter entitled "Problem 1" in S. Kierkegaard's *Fear and Trembling*.

the infidel is a justifiable act, in the same category as the execution of a criminal deserving of capital punishment, and thus is not an act of murder.

There is, however, another religious response available, and from a moral perspective it is far more appealing. Moral imperatives are themselves regarded as supremely religious principles and in many contexts are assigned greater importance than the purely ritualistic. An excellent example of this approach is the following talmudic discussion. There are three precepts, fundamental to Jewish life, which may not be violated by a Jew even when his life is threatened should he fail to comply with the demands made upon him. He may not, under any conditions, worship an idol, commit adultery or incest, or perpetrate an act of murder. These are all in the category of *yehoreg ve-al yaavor*, "one ought to submit to death rather than violate" any of these commandments. However, if a Jew sees an individual pursuing another to take his life, he must intervene to prevent the murder even to the point of taking the life of the pursuer, but if he sees someone about to worship an idol, he may not intervene by killing the would-be idol worshipper.[10] The moral principle is more imperious than the theological.

The people at the time of the Deluge in the days of Noah worshipped idols and were morally corrupt. God determined that they were irredeemably evil and had to be annihilated. Rashi notes that the reason for the devastating punishment was not that they were idol worshippers but that they practiced violence against each other.[11] The moral precept has a religious dimension that gives it greater importance than that which is distinctively religious.

---

[10] Sanhedrin 73a.
[11] Commentary on Genesis 6:11 and 13.

The book of Genesis, in its initial chapters, deals with issues of disobedience and immorality. When Adam and Eve ate of the fruit of the forbidden tree, they acted in contradiction to the Divine Will. But the murder of Abel by Cain and the morally corrupt conduct of the people of the Generation of the Deluge, also described in the early chapters, address issues that are essentially *moral*. Beginning with the command received by Abraham to leave his father's house and proceed to the land of Canaan, the book of Genesis turns to the story of the *destiny* of the Jewish people. The sequence in which these events occur has considerable significance. The implication is that Jewish destiny, which includes life in conformity to the precepts of Torah and the establishment of the people of Israel in the Holy Land, presupposes obedience to moral precepts as a prerequisite; and Judaism sees fundamental moral precepts as invested with the same sanctity as the purely religious precepts, and perhaps even more demanding.

Conclusion

How are we to define progress in the realm of ethics and morality? It is relatively easy to do so in the sciences. The goal of science is the formulation of laws and theories that will explain natural phenomena and render possible the task of predicting future events with relative precision. While there is some dispute about whether scientific laws and theories actually describe structures inherent in nature or are merely instruments useful for the task of facilitating explanation and prediction, there is no debate about the cumulative effect of the scientific enterprise. With each discovery, science moves forward on the path of progress. Progress consists in the articulation of new laws, verified by observation and experimentation, or the reformulation of old laws in the interests of increased knowledge and enhanced accuracy. The evolution of science may be regarded as an ongoing movement in the direction of the ideal of truth, and that constitutes progress.

It is one of the marks of scientific progress that there is universal agreement as to whether the formulation of a new law or theory should be counted as a scientific principle. Even though a dispute may arise initially—many protested the inclusion of the theory of relativity in the domain of science—uniformity of opinion in the scientific community is eventually reached. The acceptance of a proposed law or theory does not ultimately

193

depend upon and reflect the cultural variations of different peoples. If scientific progress is made, it is ultimately acknowledged universally.

It is otherwise with ethics and morality. In this domain, the very ideal that could point to a path of progress has not been ascertained in a manner acceptable to all. It would almost seem as if movement in these fields is a matter of proceeding from one theory of the ethical and moral ideal to the next. Is the goal human happiness? If so, is it to be defined in terms of the proper functioning of the individual, the experience of pleasure, a relationship with the Divine Being? Is the goal the introduction of moral principles in interpersonal relations? If so, are such principles deduced from a concept of human well-being, a categorical imperative, the welfare of society? It is not even clear that there is unanimity with respect to the *existence* of moral and ethical goals. According to some contemporary theories— logical positivism, for example—moral judgments are merely expressions of feeling. On this view, there is no such thing as a moral rule that can be construed as an imperative of conduct. But progress is not a process of moving *from one proposed goal to another* or the elimination of goals altogether; it consists in a movement directed *toward* a goal. It cannot be identified merely with change; it requires a directed advance. Unfortunately, with respect to moral and ethical theory, the intellectual community remains in a state of disagreement and controversy.

It is inevitable, therefore, that a theory of ethics and morality, if intended as a normative rather than a descriptive enterprise, will be presented from a specific point of view. Its study, however, may be profitable from every point of view. At the very least, a comparative study will contribute to the clarification of the theory one has adopted by distinguishing its elements from another that one finds unacceptable. Contrasting two different theories yields deeper insight into both. Now while it may be difficult, if not impossible, to present a theory of ethics and morality that will enjoy the acquiescence of all mankind, the theory expounded in this volume is one, I believe, that all Jews can adopt, notwithstanding the Jewish community's theological fragmentation and the diverse positions entertained by its various segments. In addition to the fact that the theory here presented expresses the essential components of a divinely sanctioned pattern of conduct, it has features that can appeal to all Jews who have absorbed the values of Jewish life and are prepared to rationally and objectively consider the development of the principles elaborated upon in this volume.

Further, the study of this volume's contents can contribute to moral progress, at least in the Jewish community. Note that ethical and moral progress depends on two factors. First, the fundamental concepts upon which such conduct is based need to be characterized and clarified. A failure to do so would leave uncertain the direction in which the movement of progress is to take place. Many who are verbally committed to a specific goal and are not adequately informed about its content go astray despite heroic efforts to abide by it. This is the theoretical task. But second, there is the practical requirement to delineate a series of steps needed to facilitate forward movement.

This volume focuses on the first, and perhaps the less difficult, of these tasks. Its purpose is essentially theoretical, to give an account of the Jewish ethical and moral ideal and its basic concepts, and to do so with relative precision. Progress will, of course, depend on psychological factors—the strength of will to adhere to precepts sanctioned by theoretical considerations even when they are contradicted by impulse and feeling, the exercise of self-discipline to abide by such precepts in an ongoing and consistent manner, the cultivation of a sense of satisfaction when abiding by these precepts so as to strengthen the tendency to continue to do so. The practical enterprise is the more challenging because it is more demanding, but it can be facilitated by a theoretical analysis of the concepts upon which it is based. A clear grasp of the goal and its values may well provide added incentive to initiate practical activity leading to progress. It is this hope that prompted the writing of this volume.

Index

197